ALL FOODS ARE CLEAN
and
EVERY DAY IS THE SABBATH

A RESPONSE TO DR. SAMUELE BACCHIOCCHI AND SEVENTH-DAY ADVENTISM ON ROMANS 14

By Elce-Junior "Thunder" Lauriston

Cover design by Richard Tinker

LAM Publications, LLC
1042 North Powderhorn Road
Camp Verde, Arizona 86322
928-554-1001
Dale@Ratzlaf.com
http://LifeAssuranceMinistries.com
Http://Ratzlaf.com

Library of Congress Control Number: 9781937948016

ISBN: 978-1-937948-01-6

Printed in the United States of America

TABLE OF CONTENTS

ABOUT THE AUTHOR

Elce-Junior "Thunder" Lauriston was born in Haiti, he grew up in Grand Bahama, Bahamas, and he currently resides in Jamaica. He was a prominent Seventh-day Adventist evangelist in Jamaica and the Cayman Islands, and also a theology student. In his 3rd academic year of studies (September 2015) in the School of Religion and Theology at Northern Caribbean University (NCU), a Seventh-day Adventist institution in Jamaica, he began to discover fatal flaws within the Adventist belief system and its core tenets as a result of his study of Biblical hermeneutics and New Testament Greek. The core tenets of Adventist beliefs and teachings include the Doctrine of the Investigative Judgment, the Sabbath, the authority of Ellen White's writings, dietary restrictions, a Sunday law-based view of eschatology, and the

Church's claim to be the only true church for the End Times. Lauriston discovered that these beliefs could not withstand intensive biblical and historical scrutiny. Additionally he discovered that SDA Church leaders and the professors at the university could not provide credible answers to his penetrating questions. This situation made it increasingly difficult for him to continue to believe and teach the Church's doctrines, and within six months of these discoveries, he withdrew from the seminary and from Adventism, along with his wife—Kahmal Williams-Lauriston. He remains a committed Christian and, at the writing of this book, he hopes to finish his theological training and become a Gospel minister and a theologian.

FOREWORD

Today there are fringe elements of the Christian community that wish to make salvation issues out of abstaining from eating meat and mandatory Sabbath observance. Elce "Thunder" Lauriston was one of the most dynamic Seventh-day Adventist evangelists in Jamaica in recent times. He has spoken to thousands in the popular SDA prophecy seminars and evangelistic campaigns. During his study of hermeneutics and Greek at the Seventh-day Adventist seminary at Northern Caribbean University, Jamaica, he soon discovered that the New Testament did not support the cultic doctrines of Adventism.

Lauriston researched the meaning of the "foods" and "day" spoken of in Romans 14. Utilizing the Septuagint, the Greek translation of the Hebrew Scriptures, and NT Greek, he presents strong arguments that support the fact that the Mosaic dietary restrictions and the mandatory observance of "days" have been lifted for Christians.

Utilizing these language tools, Lauriston demonstrates that Paul taught the early Christians that "all foods are clean" and abstaining from eating any meat was based on personal conviction or preference. The author also shows that the "days" which are not to be esteemed "one over the other" include the weekly Sabbath.

In this book, Lauriston evaluates the Seventh-day Adventist Church's Sabbath-friendly reading of Romans 14 and Colossians 2, as articulated by the late Dr. Samuele Bacchiocchi, and demonstrates that its position is untenable. Lauriston provides his readers with definitive answers that support the Christian's freedom in the Gospel in respect to meats and the non-necessity to observe ritual holy days-especially the Sabbath.

I am happy to recommend this book to those who want to discover the truth on these two issues and walk in its light.

Dale Ratzlaff, author of *Sabbath in Christ,* founder of Life Assurance Ministries

DEDICATION

This book is dedicated to my darling wife, Kahmal, my two lovely children, Kah-El (son) and Kah-Liyah (daughter), and my mother Ermana Lauriston. Without their love, support, dedication, encouragements, sacrifices, and patience, I would not be the man that I am becoming.

ACKNOWLEDGEMENTS

I am eternally grateful to my good friend, Kerry Wynne, for inspiring and prodding me to write this book. Undying thanks goes to my wife, Kahmal Lauriston, and children for bearing with me. They were deprived of my time and attention while I prepared the manuscript for this book. Special thanks also goes to Dale Ratzlaff for his invaluable support, mentorship, and sacrificial assistance in making this book a reality. Also I express my heart-felt gratitude to an extended group of other individuals, including Phillip Washington, Damian Skeen, Kadrian Thomas and Jenoye Stewart for helping me to keep theologically sharp, stimulated, and nurtured by the discussions that we have had. Extra special thanks goes to my sisters, Widline Lauriston, Elsie Lauriston, Betty Charles, Georgia Petitfrere, Wanda Smith, and Anastacia Forbes for encouraging me to set my standards high. I must also thank my good friends Joan Hutcheson, Samuel Brown, Marcia Hall, Marlenie Moodie, Mark and Cindy Allen, Carla Brooks, Peter and Renee Gregory, Bill and Sheila Burns, Teresa Beem, Daniel Dulcich, Michael Pursley, Dave Melton, Margie Littell, Nancy Paige, Lorna Lee, Margaret Squire, Anthony Andreola, Tony Andreola, Lena Joseph, and a host of others, for their prayers, support, and encouragement. I gratefully thank Kerry Wynne and Martin H. Klayman for assisting me with the editing of this manuscript. A huge debt of gratitude is owed to Dr. Andre Hill and Tim Martin

(The Centers for Apologetics Research, California, USA) for their critical comments, recommendations, and editorial suggestions. Last of all and greatest of all, I give thanks to my Lord and Savior Jesus Christ for giving me the mental ability and the resources to be able to make this contribution to a better understanding of the Gospel of Jesus as articulated by St. Paul.

INTRODUCTION

Romans Chapter 14 has continued to be a debatable chapter in regard to the Levitical dietary rules and the Sabbath question. The late SDA scholar, Dr. Samuele Bacchiocchi, promoted the view that this passage neither eradicates the Levitical distinction between "clean and unclean" foods (Lev. 11 and Deut. 14:1-21), nor relegates the keeping of the weekly Sabbath to that of a believer's choice. These views continue to be held by Adventism. Their polemic is that Romans 14 is speaking about days of fasting that existed in the early church-- that the discussion in this passage is in regard to the question of whether or not to avoid meats for sale that might have been ceremonially contaminated by having been offered to idols. Adventists maintain that both the Sabbath and the Levitical dietary rules are uncompromisingly binding on Christians today. Having been a Seventh-day Adventist for about a decade and a conference evangelist for about four years, I once believed this to be true and fervently taught it to thousands of individuals in the various preaching, teaching, and evangelistic platforms that the Church had provided me. However, having gotten a better understanding of the Bible, the Old and New Covenants, biblical history, hermeneutics, and being fluent in reading and understanding New Testament Greek, I was forced to discard such positions. In this book, I will demonstrate the untenable nature of these Adventist positions and explain why Christians should not concern themselves with these issues. It is my prayer that my readers will find this book supportive of Christian liberty and provide a resource in regard to questions about the relevance of dietary laws and the keeping of the Sabbath. Most of all, I pray that my readers will come to understand that in Christ, *All Foods are Clean and Every Day is the Sabbath.*

Elce-Junior "Thunder" Lauriston

OVERVIEW OF ROMANS 14

Romans 14 can be divided into two sections or paragraphs that undergird two "laws" or principles that can be observed in the chapter. Verses 1-13 can be understood as the "Law-principles of liberty" and the second section, vs. 14-23, can be seen as the "Law-principles of love." In the first section, Paul encourages the "strong" Christian to receive the "weak," who have scruples about diet and the observance of a "day," and to not show contempt towards him for his sensitive conscience (vs. 1, 3, 5). He advises the "weak" to not judge his "strong" brother, who eats anything and does not observe the day, because "God has received him" and "will make him stand" (vs. 3-4). Paul then explains that **(1)** in both of their actions, whether to eat or abstain from eating or to observe the "day," they both belong to and give thanks to God (vs. 5-6), **(2)** both of them belong "to the Lord" whether in life or in death (vs. 7-9), and **(3)** neither of them should judge each other because Christ is the ultimate Judge and it is to Him that both the weak and the strong will give an account; and by virtue of that, they should be cautious not to make each other stumble (vs. 10-13).

In the second section, "Law of Love," Paul shares his personal conviction and knowledge "in the Lord" that no food is unclean in and of itself except for the one who regards a food as unclean (vs. 14). He exhorts the "strong" one to walk in love and to not "grieve or destroy" his weak brother by what he is eating (vs. 15-16). In verses 17-19, Paul stresses the importance of things that foster Christian living, the "Kingdom of God," that is--righteousness, peace, and the joy in the Holy Spirit, "mutual up-building," and striving for peace, which approves one before God and man. Both the weak and the strong ought to strive towards this. In verses 20 and 21, Paul reiterates that "everything is clean." However, the "strong" should not destroy God's work on account of that liberty and understanding. Paul further instructs the "strong," in keeping with the principle of love (vs. 15), to not eat meat, drink wine, or do anything that will cause his "weak" brother to stumble. In verses 22-23, Paul exhorts the "strong" to keep his faith–that is, his ability to eat whatever he wants– between himself and God. Additionally he commends him for not condemning himself by living according to his convictions. At the same time, he quickly cautions the doubter (weak one) that if he doesn't eat on the basis of faith, he is condemned because "whatever does not proceed from faith is sin."

CHAPTER ONE

DR. SAMUELE BACCHIOCCHI AND THE SDA CHURCH'S POSITION ON ROMANS 14

(A) Foods in Romans 14 are not a reference to Leviticus 11 dietary laws.

Dr. Samuele Bacchiocchi and the Adventist Church hold to the view that the foods referred to in Romans 14 are not a reference to the clean and unclean animal rules of Leviticus 11 and Deuteronomy 14. They believe, rather, that these food issues were matters of "doubtful disputations" (vs. 1- KJV) or mere "quarrel over opinions" (ESV), and that these issues had nothing to do with the dietary food laws laid down by God in Leviticus and Deuteronomy. Bacchiocchi asserts that the problem that arose in Rome was, "...a fanatical (heretical) ascetic group, strikingly similar to that of Colossae, [which] advocated strict vegetarianism, abstention from wine and the observance of days (Rom. 14:1-10, 21)."[1] He further asserts that:

> ...the conflict between the "weak" and the "strong" over diet and days is only remotely related (if at all) to the Mosaic law. The "weak man" who "eats only vegetables" (14:2), drinks no wine, (14:21) and "esteems one day as better [apparently for fasting] than another" (14:5) can claim no support for such convictions from the Old Testament. Nowhere does the Mosaic law prescribe strict vegetarianism, total abstinence from wine and a preference for fasting days.[2]

In essence, Bacchiocchi finds little or no support that such asceticism can be derived from the Mosaic Law. He comments further that such asceticism may have derived from "sectarian

---

[1] Samuele Bacchiocchi, *From Sabbath to Sunday: A Historical Investigation of the Rise of Sunday Observance in Early Christianity* (Rome, Italy: The Pontifical Gregorian University Press, 1977), p. 342.

[2] Ibid, p. 343.

Judaism" and that the whole discussion "is not about freedom to observe the law versus freedom from its observance, but concerns "unessential" scruples of conscience dictated not by divine precepts but by human conventions and superstitions."[3] The Seventh-day Adventist Bible Commentary concludes concerning Romans 14 that:

> Paul, in Rom. 14, is not (1) disparaging a diet of "herbs" (vegetables), or (2) doing away with the age-old Biblical distinction between clean and unclean meats, or (3) abolishing the seventh-day Sabbath of the moral law…. The person who thus claims must read into Paul's argument something that is not there.[4]

In the official beliefs of the Seventh-day Adventist Church, an indirect but conclusive assertion is made concerning Romans 14:

> The New Testament did not abolish the distinction between clean and unclean flesh foods. Some believe that because these dietary laws are mentioned in Leviticus, they are merely ceremonial or ritualistic, so are no longer valid for Christians. Yet the distinction between clean and unclean animals dates back to Noah's day—long before Israel existed. As principles of health, these dietary laws carry with them an ongoing obligation.[5]

Not only does the Adventist Church sees the meat distinctions as an "ongoing obligation" on Christians, but its prophetess, Ellen G. White (1827-1915), goes so far as to make meat-eating a moral and spiritual issue. She posits that meat-eating will lessen one's spirituality by imparting animal instincts. She stated, "A diet of flesh meat tends to develop animalism. A development of

---

[3] Ibid, p. 344.

[4] Francis D. Nichol, The Seventh-day Adventist Bible Commentary: The Holy Bible With Exegetical and Expository Comment., Commentary Reference Series (Washington, D.C.: Review and Herald Publishing Association, 1978), p. 635.

[5] Ministerial Association General Conference of SDA, Seventh-day Adventists Believe (Boise, ID: Pacific Press Publishing Association, 1988, 2005), p. 319.

animalism lessens spirituality, rendering the mind incapable of understanding truth."[6] She ominously portends that a failure to be convicted on the matter of meat-eating will cause many to apostatize from "God's people." She says, "...Many who are now only half converted on the question of meat eating will go from God's people, to walk no more with them."[7] Evangelical Christians who read these statements by Ellen White may be left in awe and disbelief, given their general understanding of Jesus' teaching to the contrary in Mark 7 that diet does not affect one's morality nor spirituality. But Ellen White does not stop there. She takes this matter to the level of incredulity when she states that those who are waiting for Christ's Advent must eventually give up meat-eating entirely:

> Among those who are waiting for the coming of the Lord meat eating will eventually be done away; flesh will cease to form a part of their diet. We should ever keep this end in view and endeavor to work steadily toward it.[8]

She stated further:

> Will the people who are preparing to become holy, pure, and refined, that they may be introduced into *the society of heavenly angels*, continue to take the life of God's creatures and subsist on their flesh and enjoy it as a luxury? From what the Lord has shown me, this order of things will be changed, and God's peculiar people will exercise temperance in all things. . . .[9] (emphasis mine)

In no uncertain terms, Ellen White believed and exhorted that *before* Adventists are "perfected," and thus be able to stand before God, meat-eating, tea, and coffee are things that must be given up:

---

[6] Ellen G. White, *Counsels on Health* (Washington, DC: Ellen G. White Estate, Inc., 2008), p. 575.
[7] White, *Last Day Events*, p. 82.
[8] Ibid, p. 81.
[9] White, *Counsels on Health*, p. 70.

Those who have received instruction regarding the evils of the use of flesh foods, tea, and coffee, and rich and unhealthful food preparations, and who are determined to make a covenant with God by sacrifice, will not continue to indulge their appetite for food that they know to be unhealthful. God demands that the appetite be cleansed, and that self-denial be practiced in regard to those things which are not good. This is a work that will have to be done before His people can stand before Him a perfected people.[10]

These statements are suggesting that one's salvation will be affected should one decide to not give up flesh foods and certain drinks, and also abstinence therefrom is a *prerequisite for* going to heaven. These statements by Adventism's prophetess, Ellen White, are not mere theological logorrhea that can be disregarded by Seventh-day Adventists. To the contrary, her writings are believed to be "authoritative...truth" that serves to "...provide for the church comfort, guidance, instruction, and correction...."[11,12] Furthermore, before one is accepted into Adventist fellowship and membership, one must "...affirm their acceptance of the fundamental beliefs in the presence of the local congregation or other properly appointed body" by answering affirmatively a series of thirteen vows, in the form of questions, of which number eight is professing one's faith in "the gift of prophecy", which is Ellen White and her writings.[13] Based on her statements, as well as their oath-bound loyalty to Ellen White, it is not surprising that Bacchiocchi and his Church go to great lengths

[10] White, *Counsels on Diet and Foods*, p. 381.
[11] *Seventh-day Adventists Believe*, p. 247.
[12] This statement of belief has been revised and reads as, "Her writings speak with prophetic authority and provide comfort, guidance, instruction, and correction to the church." (https://www.adventist.org/en/beliefs/church/the-gift-of-prophecy/).
[13] Secretariat General Conference of Seventh-day Adventists, *Seventh-day Adventist Church Manual*, 19th Revised Ed. (Nampa, ID: Pacific Press Publishing Association, 2016), pp. 45-46. (see also *Seventh-day Adventists Believe*, pp. 247-258)

to obfuscate, reinterpret, ignore, and totally reject the clear teachings of the New Testament, particularly Romans 14, on these issues of diet and the observing of a "day" in an effort to corroborate Scripture with what she said, rather than to discard her misguided and cultic pronouncements.

(B) On The use of κοινος (*koinos*) in vs. 14

Bacchiocchi points out that the Greek word meaning "unclean foods" in the Septuagint text of Leviticus 11 is different from the Greek word Paul used for "unclean foods" in Romans 14. This difference in wording, he claims, is evidence that it is not the day and diet elements of the Law of Moses that Paul is discussing in this passage. Bacchiocchi observes:

> That the Mosaic Law is not at stake in Romans 14 is also indicated by the term *"koinos—common"* which is used in verse 14 to designate "unclean" food. This term is radically different from the word *"akathartos—impure"* used in Leviticus 11 (Septuagint) to designate unlawful foods. This suggests that the dispute was not over meat which was unlawful according to the Mosaic Law, but about meat which *per se* was lawful to eat but because of its association with idol worship (cf. 1 Cor. 8:1-13) was regarded by some as *"koinos—common,"* that is, to be avoided by Christians.[14]

So, in Dr. Bacchiocchi's mind, *koinos* is simply referring to "common," idolatrous food that Christians should avoid. If such an argument can be sustained by lexically studying the use of *koinos* and *akathartos* in the LXX as well as the NT— and if it can indeed be evinced that *koinos* merely referred to 'clean' foods that were to be avoided by their association with idolatry— Bacchiocchi would have made a profound discovery. Christians should gladly fall in line. However, if it can be demonstrated that Bacchiocchi's assessment and conclusion about *koinos* and

[14] Bacchiocchi, *The Sabbath Under Crossfire: A Biblical Analysis of Recent Sabbath/Sunday Developments* (Berrien Springs, MI: *Biblical Perspectives*, 1999), p.240.

akathartos cannot be sustained, then such a notion should be discarded at once.

On the use of the word *koinos*, the *Seventh-day Adventist Bible Commentary* does not go into much detail but merely states, "**Unclean.** Gr. *koinos*, literally, "common." This term was used to describe those things which, though "common" to the world, were forbidden to the pious Jew...."[15] This assessment is so vague that it raises more questions than it answers. Exactly what was "common" to the world but was "forbidden to the pious Jew?" It certainly wasn't the ordinary activities of daily living! It would have to be things that tend to set Jews apart from gentiles.

There is, unfortunately, a reason for Adventism's avoidance of a deeper and broader analysis of the exegetical and lexical details of the word *koinos*. They have surreptitiously redefined and narrowed its meaning, but this shallow position cannot bear scrutiny. In the coming pages this fact will be demonstrated sufficiently.

(C) Bacchiocchi's and Adventism's position on the "Weak" Believer, Days of Fasting, and Ceremonial Days

Bacchiocchi believes that Paul could not have been referring to Sabbath-keepers as the "weak" since Paul himself was a Sabbath-keeper. And also, to the contrary, Paul considered himself "strong." He states:

> Finally, if as generally presumed, it was the "weak" believer who observed the Sabbath, Paul would classify himself with the "weak" since he observed the Sabbath and other Jewish feasts (Acts 18:4, 19;

---

[15] Nichol, *The Seventh-day Adventist Bible Commentary: The Holy Bible With Exegetical and Expository Comment.*, Commentary Reference Series, p. 639.

17:1, 10, 17; 20:16). Paul, however, views himself as "strong" ("we who are strong"—Rom 15:1); thus, he could not have been thinking of Sabbath-keeping when he speaks of the preference over days. [16]

Having made this observation about Paul, Bacchiocchi then posits that the "day" referred to in Romans 14 could not be "feast days," — i.e. the Sabbath, but "fast days:"

> The preference over days in Romans presumably had to do with fast-days rather than feast-days, since the context deals with abstinence from meat and wine (Rom. 14:2, 6, 21). Support for this view is provided by the *Didache* (Ch. 8) which enjoins Christians to fast on Wednesday and Friday rather than on Monday and Thursday like the Jews. Paul refuses to deliberate on such private matters such as fasting, because he recognizes that spiritual exercises can be performed in different ways by different people. [17]

Bacchiocchi's assumption that Paul upheld Sabbath-keeping led him to speculate that a two-verse treatment of the subject would have been insufficient to address an "inflammatory" subject such as the Sabbath. He maintains that those were specific days of fasting, and thus should be left to one's own conviction:

> If the conflict in the Roman Church had been over the observance of holy days, the problem would have been even more manifest than the one over diet. After all, eating habits are a private matter, but Sabbath-keeping is a public, religious exercise of the whole community. Any disagreement on the latter would have been not only noticeable but also inflammatory. The fact that Paul devotes 21 verses to the discussion of food and less than two verses (Rom. 14:5-6) to very limited problem for the Roman Church, presumably because it had to do with private conviction on the merit or demerit of doing certain spiritual exercises such as fasting on some specific days. [18]

Bacchiocchi then concludes that Romans 14 may well be referring to "certain days" that the Romans superstitiously thought were

---

[16] Bacchiocchi, *The Sabbath Under Crossfire*, p. 241.

[17] Bacchiocchi, *The Sabbath in the New Testament: Answers to Questions* (Berrien Springs, MI: *Biblical Perspectives*, 2000), p. 84.

[18] Ibid, pp. 84-85.

better to undertake "specific projects" and that it is hardly probable that the Sabbath is in view in vs. 5:

> In the Roman world there was a superstitious belief that certain days were more favorable than others for undertaking some specific projects. The Early Fathers frequently rebuked Christians for adopting such a superstitious mentality. It is possible that Paul alludes to this kind of problem, which at his time, however, was still too small to deserve much attention. In the light of the above consideration, we conclude that it is hardly probable that the Sabbath is included in the "days" of Romans 14:5.[19]

The *Seventh-day Adventist Bible Commentary* assumes that the "day" referred to in Romans 14:5 referred to "special days" and "ceremonial days," excluding the Sabbath, and it is these days and their observance that are to be left to individual conviction. Having made that assumption about the "day," this comment is given with regards to the "weak" and the "strong" believer:

> Those believers whose faith enables them immediately to leave behind all ceremonial holidays should not despise others whose faith is less strong. Nor, in turn, may the latter criticize those who seem to them lax. Each believer is responsible to God (Rom. 14:10–12). And what God expects of each of His servants is that he shall "be fully persuaded in his own mind" and conscientiously follow his convictions in accordance with the light he has received and understood so far.[20]

---

[19] Ibid, p. 85.

[20] Nichol, *The Seventh-day Adventist Bible Commentary: The Holy Bible With Exegetical and Expository Comment.*, p. 637.

CHAPTER TWO

DIETARY RULES OF LEVITICUS 11
AND DEUTERONOMY 14 ARE ABOLISHED

(A) The Mosaic Law is in view in Romans 14

The argument by Bacchiocchi and Adventism that the Mosaic Law is not in view nor at stake in Romans 14 is not sound, nor is it based on the internal evidences. His assumption that Romans 14 is referring to "asceticism" that may have been promoted by "sectarian Judaism" cannot be derived from the passage under consideration. Looking at the passage and its *immediate* context, it is easy to see that the Mosaic Law[21] is what Paul is *directly* discussing. The context of Romans 14 actually begins with 13:8 and ends with 15:13. This forms an exhortative pericope[22] to

---

[21] The Mosaic Law is the entire Pentateuch (Genesis to Deuteronomy) and it contains moral laws, ceremonial laws, statute laws, and civil laws. Adventism maintains that the Ten Commandments are God's "Moral Law" and they "convey God's pattern of conduct for humanity." (*Seventh-day Adventists Believe*, p. 264). It places great emphasis on the Ten Commandments and believes that they all are moral laws in an effort to safeguard and universalize mandatory Sabbath-keeping. While the Ten Commandments do contain moral laws, yet it cannot be said that they are entirely "moral laws," as the Sabbath is clearly a ceremonial law. This point will be proven beyond a doubt in chapter 4. Additionally, Adventism creates a false dichotomy between the "Law of God" (Ten Commandments) and the "Law of Moses" (Book of the Law) in an effort to maintain mandatory Sabbath-keeping, but this dichotomy does not exist in Scripture. The Law is a unit and has various names. The Book of Nehemiah reveals the various names that the Law was recognized by, i.e., "the Law" (Neh. 8:2, 7, 9, 13; 10:36; 12:44; 13:3), "the Book of the Law" (Neh. 8:3), "the Law of God" (Neh. 8:8; 10:28), "the Book of the Law of God" (Neh. 8:18), "the Book of the Law of the Lord" (Neh. 9:3), "God's Law that was given by Moses" (Neh. 10:29), "the Book of Moses" (Neh. 13:1), and "Law that the LORD had commanded by Moses" (8:14).

[22] A section of text forming a coherent thought.

Jewish and gentile Christians,[23] who had considerable differences with regards to diet and days, to "love one another" despite their differences. After commanding them to love each other, Paul describes how to show this love, with respect to their inherent disagreement about diet and days (14:1-15:7) and thus "fulfil the Law." This understanding is resident in chapter 14 because as Paul instructs both the "weak" and the "strong" brother, he says to the "strong" that if he causes his "weak" brother to be grieved by his food, he is "no longer walking in love" (vs. 15). In Romans 13:1-7, Paul explains a Christian's duty and attitude towards worldly governments, then in vs. 8 exhorts, "Owe no one anything, except to love each other, for the one who loves another has fulfilled the law." Now, what law is Paul referring to here when he says that the one who loves another has fulfilled the law? We need not go outside of the text for the answer because Paul adequately provides the answer. In 13:9, Paul quotes four commandments from Exodus 20 (found also in Deut. 5) and one from Leviticus 19, and then he packaged the entire Mosaic Law in the category of "any other commandment" to define what Law he is talking about. We read, "For the commandments, "You shall not commit adultery, You shall not murder, You shall not steal, You shall not covet," and any other commandment, are summed up in this word: "You shall love your neighbor as yourself." Having referred to the law in this way, Paul then concludes in vs. 10, "Love does no wrong to a neighbor; therefore love is the fulfilling of the law." In several other places in the New Testament, we read of the entire Mosaic Law being referred to in this manner and also that it is fulfilled by 'loving our neighbors as ourselves.' In Matthew 22, a proficient Jewish lawyer asked Jesus what he thought was a profound question: "Teacher, which is the great commandment in

---

[23] The immediate audience of the Book of Romans is Jewish and gentile Christians in Rome (Rom. 1:14, 16; 2:9, 14,17; 3:29-30; 9:30-31; 10:12; chap. 11; 15:8-12, etc.)

the Law?"(22:36). Jesus responded "You shall love the Lord your God with all your heart and with all your soul and with all your mind. This is the great and first commandment. And a second is like it: You shall love your neighbor as yourself." (vs. 37-39). Then Jesus concludes in vs. 40, "On these two commandments depend all the Law and the Prophets."[24] We find a similar statement (to that of Rom. 13:8-10) made by Paul in Galatians 5 concerning the Law. There, in vs. 14, he states, "For the whole law is fulfilled in one word: "You shall love your neighbor as yourself." James reiterates the same principle in his epistle when he said, "If you really fulfil the royal law according to the Scripture, "You shall love your neighbor as yourself," you are doing well." (2:8). And James is very clear that he is speaking about the "whole law" (vs. 9-11). From these examples, we can see, beyond any doubt, that the whole Mosaic Law is what's in view in Romans 14. This is further illustrated as Paul talks about "clean and unclean" foods (vs. 14, 20), "observing a day" (vs. 5-6) (both of which were huge issues to Jews and which are discussed in detail in the Mosaic Law), and his clear reference to the "Scriptures" (the Old Testament) in 15:4.[25]

We can also observe a beautiful transition into the subject matter in 13:11-14:1. In vs. 11 and 12 of chapter 13, Paul exhorts the believers to wake up from their sleep (spiritual stupor and inactivity), to put on the "armor of light," and to cast off the works of darkness because salvation and the Day (of Christ's coming) is near. In vs. 13-14 he continues, "Let us walk properly as in the daytime, not in orgies and drunkenness, not in sexual

---

[24] "The Law and the Prophets" is the NT's designation for the entire Old Testament, sometimes with slight variations in nomenclature (Matt. 5:17; 7:12; 11:13; Luke 16:16; 24:44; John 1:45; Acts 13:15; 24:14; 28:23; and Rom. 3:21)

[25] The New Testament's use of the term "Scripture" or "Scriptures" primarily refers to the Old Testament, as the majority of the New Testament weren't penned as yet and neither was the canon of the NT completed and closed. (Matt. 22:29; Matt. 26:54, 56; Luke 24:27, 32, 45; John 5:39; 10:35; Acts 15:21; 17:2, 11; 18:28; Gal. 4:30; 2 Tim. 3:15-17; etc.)

immorality and sensuality, not in quarrelling and jealousy. But put on the Lord Jesus Christ, and make no provision for the flesh, to gratify its desires." As Paul continues to exhort these Christians and to explain to them how to "love and fulfil the Law," he tells them how they should not walk ('in darkness') and how they should walk, by putting on Christ.

Notice carefully that one of the ways that Paul tells them not to live is "in quarrelling." This is important to note because as we read 14:1, we see Paul urging the "strong" to "receive as a Christian brother", such is the thrust of the Greek word προσλαμβάνεσθε (proslambanesthe), the one whose faith is weak and that he should not have "quarrels over opinions." And without allowing us to guess as to what these 'opinionated quarrels' were about, Paul goes on to elaborate on two *divisive points* in the Mosaic Law, which are diet and a "day," while explaining to them how to maintain their individual Christian liberty and coexist, and at the same time "fulfil the Law" by "walking in love." Right away, we can detect that Bacchiocchi's assertion that Romans 14 is alluding to or condemning "asceticism" that may have been promoted by "sectarian Judaism" is not based on sound exegesis, but from mere conjecture or evasive sophistry. The exegetical evidence stands resolute: Romans 14 is referring to the Mosaic Law and those two divisive problems therein—diet and the Sabbath.

(B) Can abstinence from wine, strict vegetarianism, and "esteeming one day above another" be supported from the Old Testament?

Bacchiocchi appears to side-track his readers by observing that the one who promoted abstinence from wine, practiced veganism, and esteemed one "fasting" day above another in Romans 14 cannot find support for his convictions in the Old Testament. In the first case, he is only partly correct, and in the second case what he said is true but irrelevant. Of course there are no Old Testament instructions regarding fasting days. There are, however, specific and detailed instructions for esteeming the days of appointed festivals, including the weekly Sabbath. These days are the only kind of days in Judaism to be greatly esteemed. It is no wonder that Bacchiocchi wants to discuss days of fasting.

One will not read in the Law where total abstinence from wine (with the exception of priests when ministering in the Tabernacle and Nazirites)[26] is enjoined upon Jews. Neither will one observe in

---

[26] After the two sons of Aaron were killed by God for offering "strange fire" to Him, we find this instruction concerning priests in Leviticus 10:8 "And the LORD spoke to Aaron, saying, 9 "Drink no wine or strong drink, you or your sons with you, when you go into the tent of meeting, lest you die. It shall be a statute forever throughout your generations. 10 You are to distinguish between the holy and the common, and between the unclean and the clean, 11 and you are to teach the people of Israel all the statutes that the LORD has spoken to them by Moses." This was not an absolute ban on wine and strong drinks for the priestly caste because the passage says that it's *when* they are going to minister in the Tabernacle that they had to abstain from wine; this is explicitly stated in Ezekiel 44:21 "No priest shall drink wine when he enters the inner court." But outside of their ministerial duties, they were permitted to drink wine (Num. 18:8-14; Deut. 18:1-5). Nazirites represented the second class of Jews not permitted to drink wine. Individuals who took a Naziritic vow were not allowed to drink wine as long as they are *under the vow*, but when the vow was terminated, they were permitted to resume drinking wine (Num. 6:1-6). A third class of Jews who were not permitted to drink wine was the Rechabites, whose

the Mosaic Law where vegetarianism is *explicitly* enjoined. However, this fact does not rule out the fact that under certain circumstances the Jews could be virtually forced to adopt a vegetarian diet, at least temporarily. This potential situation is clearly supported by the Mosaic Law in view of the fact that eating food offered to idols is forbidden. With respect to strict vegetarianism and total abstinence from wine, it is best that I deal with both issues as one because they pertain to diet and correlate in Judaic dietary matters.

In the Mosaic Law, idolatry is condemned in the most explicit way. In Exodus 20, two of the commandments that form the heart of the covenant between God and Israel forbade idolatry (Exo. 20:3-6).[27] In Leviticus 19:4, Israel is warned to not turn aside to idols nor make metallic gods. In Deuteronomy 12:29-31, Israel is charged by Moses to not be ensnared by the gods of the people of the land that they are about to dispossess, and neither should they, "inquire about their gods, saying, 'How did these nations serve their gods?—that I also may do the same.'" In Deuteronomy 32:37-38, we see where wine and foods (as sacrifices) can be associated with idolatry when they are used as offerings to idols. This last text provides a profound insight with regards to meat and wine when they are used in idolatrous worship. As a matter of fact, Exodus 32 states explicitly that food and drink were connected with the Golden Calf incident and idolatry. In vs. 6 we read, "And they rose up early the next day and offered burnt offerings and brought peace offerings. And the people sat down to eat and drink and rose up to play." In his comment on this issue

---

father Jonadab enjoined upon them, "You shall not drink wine, neither you nor your sons forever" (see Jer. 35).

[27] The Ten Commandments are the very words of the Old Covenant between God and Israel (Exo. 34:27-28; Deut. 4:13; 5:2-22; 9:9-11)

in 1 Corinthians 10, Paul directly calls this idolatry: "Do not be idolaters as some of them were; as it is written, "The people sat down to eat and drink and rose up to play." (vs. 7). In Numbers 25, we can observe again where food is directly connected with idolatry, when it is used in that context. Numbers 25 states, "While Israel lived in Shittim, the people began to whore with the daughters of Moab. These invited the people to the sacrifices of their gods, and the people ate and bowed down to their gods. So Israel yoked himself to Baal of Peor. And the anger of the LORD was kindled against Israel." (vs. 1-3). The Psalmist, commenting on and reciting this incident in Psalm 106, adds, "Then they yoked themselves to the Baal of Peor, and ate sacrifices offered to the dead...." (vs. 28).

From these incidences cited, we see clearly how one can commit idolatry with regards to "food and wine." In light of this, the question must be asked, can situations like these drive a conscientious Jew to "strict vegetarianism"? The answer is a resounding, Yes! If a Jew is placed in a situation where he is aware that food or wine (which he could otherwise have eaten under normal circumstances) was used to worship an idol, by the direct teaching of the Law, he will be forced to refuse such articles of food lest he commit idolatry.

If that Jew lives in an environment where idolatry is the norm or prevalent, we can readily see how such a situation would force him to opt for "strict vegetarianism" to ensure that he is not polluted. Astonishingly, we find this to be the exact situation with Daniel and his friends in Babylon! In Daniel 1:5 we read that, "The king assigned them a daily portion of the food that the king ate, and of the wine that he drank...." But instead of partaking of the king's provision, we read in vs. 8 that, "...Daniel resolved that he would not defile himself with the king's food, or with the wine that he drank. Therefore he asked the chief of the eunuchs to allow him not to defile himself."

For what reason did Daniel and his friends make this resolve? John Wesley provides some good insights in his *Explanatory Notes Upon the Old Testament*:

> There may be several weighty reasons assigned why *Daniel* did this. 1. Because many of those meats provided for the king's table, were forbidden by the *Jewish* law. 2. *Daniel* knew these delicacies would too much gratify the flesh. 3. He did not dare to eat and drink things consecrated to idols. 4. He was sensible, how unsuitable delicate fare would be to the afflicted state of God's people. Therefore he was herein a rare pattern of avoiding all the occasions of evil.[28]

John MacArthur, Jr., elucidates further:

> The pagan food and drink was devoted to idols. To indulge was to be understood as honoring these deities. Daniel "purposed in his heart" (cf. Prov. 4:23) not to engage in compromise by being untrue to God's call of commitment (cf. Ex. 34:14, 15). Also, foods that God's law prohibited (Lev. 11:1) were items that pagans consumed; to partake entailed direct compromise (cf. Dan. 1:12).[29]

Additionally, Daniel and his friends were not vegetarians nor did they practice abstinence from wine (Dan. 10:3; cf. Deut. 14:22-27; Psa. 104:14-15). However, being placed in such a *non-kosher environment* where the food and wine were defiled by paganism and idolatry, Daniel's only possible response, in view of the requirements of the Mosaic Law, was strict vegetarianism. In Daniel 1:11-12 we read, "Then Daniel said to the steward whom the chief of the eunuchs had assigned over Daniel, Hananiah, Mishael, and Azariah, "Test your servants for ten days; let us be

---

[28] John Wesley, *Explanatory Notes Upon the Old Testament, Volume 3* (Bristol: William Pine, 1765), p. 2431.

[29] John MacArthur, Jr., ed., *The MacArthur Study Bible*, electronic ed. (Nashville, TN: Word Pub., 1997), p. 1227.

given vegetables to eat and water to drink." The duress of the situation propelled Daniel and his friends to adjust to a vegan diet in order to obey God, the Mosaic Law, and not "defile" their sensitive consciences, lest they countenance idolatry. This is not mere "asceticism" in the minds of conscientious Jews; this is loyalty to God and His Law.

Antiochus IV Epiphanes (175-164 B.C.) attempted to destroy the Jewish laws and force the Jews to commit idolatry through these same issues of food and drink. We learn in I Maccabees, that many Jews opted to die rather than yield to his demands.[30] Even though the text does not state that they became vegetarians, it is a reasonable assumption that many of them did, given the

---

[30] 1 Maccabees 1:41-50, 59-64 - Moreover king Antiochus wrote to his whole kingdom, that all should be one people, 42 And every one should leave his laws: so all the heathen agreed according to the commandment of the king. 43 Yea, many also of the Israelites consented to his religion, and sacrificed unto idols, and profaned the sabbath. 44 For the king had sent letters by messengers unto Jerusalem and the cities of Judah that they should follow the strange laws of the land, 45 And forbid burnt offerings, and sacrifice, and drink offerings, in the temple; and that they should profane the sabbaths and festival days: 46 And pollute the sanctuary and holy people: 47 Set up altars, and groves, and chapels of idols, and sacrifice swine's flesh, and unclean beasts: 48 That they should also leave their children uncircumcised, and make their souls abominable with all manner of uncleanness and profanation: 49 To the end they might forget the law, and change all the ordinances. 50 And whosoever would not do according to the commandment of the king, he said, he should die... 59 Now the five and twentieth day of the month they did sacrifice upon the idol altar, which was upon the altar of God. 60 At which time according to the commandment they put to death certain women, that had caused their children to be circumcised. 61 And they hanged the infants about their necks, and rifled their houses, and slew them that had circumcised them. 62 Howbeit many in Israel were fully resolved and confirmed in themselves not to eat any unclean thing. 63 Wherefore they rather to die, that they might not be defiled with meats, and that they might not profane the holy covenant: so then they died. 64 And there was very great wrath upon Israel.
(The Apocrypha: King James Version (Bellingham, WA: Logos Research Systems, Inc., 1995), 1 Mac 1:41-50, 59–64.)

widespread idolatrous practices of that time and the deliberate attempts and persecutions they faced by the king and his subjects to get them to forsake the Mosaic Law.

If the Jews of Antiochus' day were so committed to the Law that they were willing to die rather than commit sacrilege, my assumption that they probably became vegetarians is not farfetched. The situation of Daniel and his friends was not nearly as precarious as that of the Jews in Antiochus' time, yet they became vegetarians. Therefore, is it possible that a comparable situation existed in Rome that would have driven the "weak" Jewish Christian to "eat vegetables"[31] and abstain from wine in order not to "defile" himself, and which also would cause him to "judge" his "strong" gentile brother who "eats all things" and does not have such scruples? That question will be explored now.

Randall A. Weiss describes, with profound insight, the environment that surrounded Jews in Rome in NT times when he said:

> Identifying the primary complement of Jewish groups within Judaism at the time of Jesus requires some understanding of the social situation within which those Jews existed. It was not a world dominated by Jews or Christians. Their environment was saturated with pagan religious influences of Rome. The Jews survived as a uniquely monotheistic moral structure in an immoral world. Granted, there were several different categories of Jews, it was still a pagan

---

[31] The Greek word used for "vegetables/herbs" in Romans 14:2 is λαχανον ("lachanon", cf. Mark 4:32; Luke 11:42) whereas the one that is used in Daniel 1:12 (LXX) is σπερμα ("sperma"-meaning "something sown," "seed"), the Hebrew equivalent of zeroa (meaning "something sown," "seed," "vegetables"). Even though they are two different words, they bear no difference in meaning. They are synonyms (cf. Matt. 13:32, where both words are used to describe the two stages of vegetation). Another synonymous Greek word for σπερμα and λαχανον is βοτανη (botane) and it is used once in the NT in Heb. 6:7 (cf. Matt. 13:32).

world system which surrounded them.[32]

Edward F. Murphy adds to the discussion, by saying:

> The entire New Testament world was engulfed in idolatry and its accompanying sexual immorality. Temple prostitution was rampant. Some of the pagan religious rites were even more immoral than those of the Old Testament pagan nations including the Canaanites. Rome ruled the world, but the Greek culture dominated. Greece had its pantheon of high gods and its innumerable lower gods and spirits. Rome took the Greek pantheon as its own and added its own maze of lower gods and spirits and those of all the peoples it conquered.[33]

Living in a pagan environment, while attempting to comply with the Law of Moses, it should not be difficult for us to grasp why the Jewish Christians in Rome were so scrupulous. Even the "clean" meats of Leviticus 11 and Deuteronomy 14 might still be ceremonially unclean. This situation is possible because these "biologically clean" meats, which were typically available for sale in the markets, might have been used in a pagan religious ceremony (cf. 1 Cor. 8; 10:25-32). A situation like this would certainly move Christians who had come out of Judaism into a vegetarian lifestyle. With this in mind, we can read with fresh understanding the following verses in Romans 14:1-4:

> As for the one who is weak in faith, welcome him, but not to quarrel over opinions. 2 One person believes he may eat anything, while the weak person eats only vegetables. 3 Let not the one who eats despise the one who abstains, and let not the one who abstains pass judgment on the one who eats, for God has welcomed him. 4 Who are you to pass judgment on the servant of another? It is before his own master that he stands or falls. And he will be upheld, for the Lord is able to make him stand.

---

[32] Randall A. Weiss, *Jewish Sects of the New Testament Era* (Cedar Hill, TX: CrossTalk, 1994), chap. I, n. p.

[33] Edward F. Murphy, *Handbook for Spiritual Warfare* (Nashville: Thomas Nelson, 1996), p. 162.

Bacchiocchi formulates an idea that might be "true" in isolation but which is false in its contextual irrelevance in this specific application. His conclusion that the "weak man" who "eats only vegetables" (14:2), drinks no wine, (14:21) and "esteems one day as better [apparently for fasting] than another" (14:5) can claim no support for such convictions from the Old Testament," is faulty and factually erroneous.

We have already proven that his conclusion about vegetables and wine is wrong. Now we will examine if "esteeming one day above another" can be supported from the Old Testament, and also if that "day" is possibly the Sabbath.

(C) The Sabbath is 'esteemed' above other days.

The word "esteem"[34] implies that its object possesses special attributes that are worthy of a high degree of respect. The Jewish sacred days have these attributes, and of all of these appointed festivals, the weekly Sabbath has such holy attributes that the Law of Moses required that two spotless lambs be sacrificed upon it (Num. 28:9-10). Ordinary days of the week do not have any attributes that possess significant worthiness. If Paul were concerned that the Christians at Rome liked to fast on certain ordinary days of the week more than on other ordinary days of the week, he would likely have worded his statement something like, "I am sorry to hear that you have gone back to preferring some fast days over other fast days." But Paul never hinted at such a situation nor made such a statement.

Exodus 16 tells of Israel's first encounter with the Sabbath in Scripture (cf. Neh. 9:13-14). In this first-ever encounter, we see clearly that it was "esteemed" above other days. In verses 25 & 26 we read: "Moses said, 'Eat it today, for today is a Sabbath to the LORD; today you will not find it in the field. Six days you shall gather it, but on the seventh day, which is a Sabbath, there will be none.'" The Manna was to fall for six days, but would cease on the seventh day because it was God's Sabbath. These newly liberated slaves were not accustomed to resting nor to regarding the seventh day of the week above other days (while enslaved in Egypt, they actually were accustomed to a ten day weekly cycle, not a seven[35]), so some of them persisted in gathering the Manna

---

[34] The Greek word used for "esteems" in Romans 14:5 is κρινω (krino), "to separate, to pick out, select, to approve, esteem, to judge, etc.," carries that connotation in this context.

[35] "...the Egyptian week was one of 10 days...." (E. W. Maunder, "Astrology" In, in *The International Standard Bible Encyclopaedia*, Volumes 1–5, ed. James Orr, John L. Nuelsen, Edgar Y. Mullins and Morris O. Evans (Chicago: The Howard-Severance Company, 1915), p. 299.)

upon it, despite the warning. The account in Exodus 16 informs us:

> On the seventh day some of the people went out to gather, but they found none. And the LORD said to Moses, "How long will you refuse to keep my commandments and my laws? See! The LORD has given you the Sabbath; therefore on the sixth day he gives you bread for two days. Remain each of you in his place; let no one go out of his place on the seventh day." So the people rested on the seventh day. (vs. 27-30).

Immediately, we see that the seventh day, which became the Sabbath, was "esteemed" to be above other days because of what God commanded. At the giving of the Law on Mt. Sinai, we also read of the seventh day's elevation above other days. Exodus 20 states:

> "Remember the Sabbath day, to keep it holy. Six days you shall labor, and do all your work, but the seventh day is a Sabbath to the LORD your God. On it you shall not do any work, you, or your son, or your daughter, your male servant, or your female servant, or your livestock, or the sojourner who is within your gates." (vs. 8-10).

With just two passages the position of Dr. Bacchiocchi and the Adventist Church collapses. But in order to satisfy your mind that the special "days" of Israel,[36] especially the weekly Sabbath, were regarded "above" other days, I will supply more evidence. In Exodus 31:12-17, we discover more how "esteemed" the Sabbath was to a Jew. It was the special, *covenantal sign* between God and Israel (vs. 13, 17). It was Israel's sign of being set apart from everyone else for God's holy use (vs. 13; cf. Eze. 20:12, 20). It was holy to God and to them (vs. 14, 15). The Israelite who ventured to work on it should be put to death and be severed from the covenant people (vs. 14, 15; 35:2; cf. Num. 15:32-36). The

---

[36] See Leviticus 23 and Numbers 28-29 for the complete list of Israel's holy days that were "esteemed" above other days. Given the nature of this polemic, with regards to the "day" in Romans 14:5-6, attention will be given exclusively to the Sabbath.

Israelites were to "observe" it as a lasting covenant throughout their generations (vs. 13, 16). Exodus 34:21 reveals that Israel could not plow nor harvest crops on the Sabbath. Chapter 35:3 says that no fire should be kindled on the Sabbath. Leviticus 23:2-3 says that the Sabbath was one of God's feasts and one of the holy convocations.

In Deuteronomy 5:12 and 15, Israel was commanded to "observe" the Sabbath as a reminder of their redemption from Egyptian slavery. In the Prophets, we see Israel being *constantly rebuked* for not "esteeming" the Sabbath above other days! In Isaiah 56, Israel is called 'blind watchmen, dumb, slumbering, and greedy dogs, shepherds without understanding, etc.,' who will face God's judgment for dis-esteeming the Sabbath. At the same time, God promised to bless the foreigner and eunuch who join themselves to Him and His covenant and esteem it. In Isaiah 58, they were castigated for not keeping and esteeming the Sabbath properly. In Jeremiah 17:19-27, Israel was lambasted for working and "bearing loads on the Sabbath" and were threatened with destruction and captivity if they did not desist and "esteem" it above other days. In Ezekiel, the priests and the nation of Israel were chaffed for profaning and disregarding the Sabbath (20:16, 21, 24; 22:8, 26; 23:38).

In Hosea 2:11, God promised to "put an end" to Israel's Sabbaths due to apostasy and moral laxity. In Amos 8, one of the reasons that God brought swift judgment on Israel was for "trading" on the Sabbath (vs. 5 -NKJV)). As a matter of fact, one of the reasons that God delivered Israel into Babylonian captivity (circa 587 B.C.) was because of their 'dis-esteeming' the Sabbath (2 Chron. 36:15-21; Jer. 17:19-27; Neh. 13:17-18). When they had returned from the Exile and quickly lapsed into dis-esteeming it, Nehemiah, fearing more punishment from God because of it, initiated many Sabbath reforms so that it could be rightly 'esteemed' (Neh. 10:28-33; 13:15-22).

During the Maccabean Era (2nd Century B.C.), thousands of Jews lost their lives because they were adamant that the Sabbath is "above" other days and they esteemed it, despite the threats from King Antiochus and the persecutions they faced.[37] Countless thousands of them were slaughtered for refusing to engage in combat on the Sabbath and thus defile it.[38]

Having examined these biblical and historical evidences, we can

---

[37] 1 Maccabees 1: 41-46, 57-58- 41 "Moreover king Antiochus wrote to his whole kingdom, that all should be one people, 42 And every one should leave his laws: so all the heathen agreed according to the commandment of the king. 43 Yea, many also of the Israelites consented to his religion, and sacrificed unto idols, and profaned the sabbath. 44 For the king had sent letters by messengers unto Jerusalem and the cities of Judah that they should follow the strange laws of the land, 45 And forbid burnt offerings, and sacrifice, and drink offerings, in the temple; and that they should profane the sabbaths and festival days: 46 And pollute the sanctuary and holy people: 57 And whosoever was found with any the book of the testament, or if any committed to the law, the king's commandment was, that they should put him to death. 58 Thus did they by their authority unto the Israelites every month, to as many as were found in the cities."

[38] 1 Maccabees 2:31 "Now when it was told the king's servants, and the host that was at Jerusalem, in the city of David, that certain men, who had broken the king's commandment, were gone down into the secret places in the wilderness, 32 They pursued after them a great number, and having overtaken them, they camped against them, and made war against them on the sabbath day. 33 And they said unto them, Let that which ye have done hitherto suffice; come forth, and do according to the commandment of the king, and ye shall live. 34 But they said, We will not come forth, neither will we do the king's commandment, to profane the sabbath day. 35 So then they gave them the battle with all speed. 36 Howbeit they answered them not, neither cast they a stone at them, nor stopped the places where they lay hid; 37 But said, Let us die all in our innocency: heaven and earth will testify for us, that ye put us to death wrongfully. 38 So they rose up against them in battle on the sabbath, and they slew them, with their wives and children and their cattle, to the number of a thousand people."
(The Apocrypha: King James Version (Bellingham, WA: Logos Research Systems, Inc., 1995), 1 Mac 2:31–38.)

confidently conclude that Bacchiocchi and Adventism have erred in asserting that the days to be esteemed or not to be esteemed are days of fasting. Even though Bacchiocchi twists the "day" to refer to "fasting," the plethora of evidences prove that the Sabbath is in Paul's view. His "fast day" theory of Romans 14 will be further disproved later in a section where we will review where the word "fasting" occurs in the New Testament and which Greek words are used in the original language. As this section closes, let me emphasize that the Jewish conviction with regards to the Sabbath being "above" other days did not change in the New Testament. We can observe a *continuous chain of conviction* about the Sabbath being above other days from the Old Testament, the Intertestamental Period, and into the New Testament. Throughout Jesus' ministry, we constantly see Him in conflict with the Jewish religious leaders because of His treating the Sabbath like "other days." A casual reading of Matthew 12:1-14, Mark 2:23-28, Luke 13:10-17, John 5:8-18 and 9:1-16 will sufficiently reveal this. In the New Testament Era, the Rabbis were so enamored with the Sabbath, and saw it as above other days, that they thought that God "wedded" the Sabbath to Israel, and concocted scrupulous rules for observing it, to the point of making it overbearing and virtually impractical. Alfred Edersheim observes:

> 'All the days of the week,' the Rabbis say, 'has God paired, except the Sabbath, which is alone, that it may be wedded to Israel.' Israel was to welcome the Sabbath as a bride; its advent as that of a king. But in practice all this terribly degenerated. Readers of the New Testament know how entirely, and even cruelly, the spirit and object of the Sabbath were perverted by the traditions of 'the elders.' But those only who have studied the Jewish law on the subject can form any adequate conception of the state of matters. Not to speak of the folly of attempting to produce joy by prescribed means, nor of the incongruousness of those means, considering the sacred character of the day, the almost numberless directions about avoiding work must have made a due observance of the Sabbath-rest the greatest labor of all. All work was arranged under thirty-nine chief classes, or "fathers,"

each of them having ever so many 'descendants,' or subordinate divisions. Thus, 'reaping' was one of the 'fathers,' or chief classes, and 'plucking ears of corn' one of its descendants. So far did this punctiliousness go that it became necessary to devise ingenious means to render the ordinary intercourse of life possible, and to evade the inconvenient strictness of the law which regulated a 'Sabbath-day's journey.'[39]

With these biblical and historical facts in mind, it should not be difficult for us to understand why there would be a controversy among Jewish and gentile Christians in Rome about a "day," and also the clear meaning and implication of Romans 14:5-6.

(D) Κοινος (*koinos*) and ακαθαρτος (*akathartos*) are interchangeable synonyms (a direct reference to Lev. 11 and Jewish dietary laws)

The Seventh-day Adventist Bible Commentary offers no help in understanding *koinos* in Romans 14:14. In fact, its content is actually detrimental as a result of its vague obfuscation. For verse 20, a key phrase is completely avoided. Bacchiocchi, on the other hand, drew a decisive conclusion:

> That the Mosaic Law is not at stake in Romans 14 is also indicated by the term *koinos*—common which is used in verse 14 to designate "unclean" food. This term is radically different from the word *akathartos*—impure used in Leviticus 11 (Septuagint) to designate unlawful foods. This suggests that the dispute was not over meat which was unlawful according to the Mosaic Law, but about meat which per se was lawful to eat but because of its association with idol worship (cf. 1 Cor. 8:1-13) was regarded by some as *koinos*—"common," that is, to be avoided by Christians.[40]

For some strange reason, Bacchiocchi seems to have gone out of

---

[39] Alfred Edersheim, *The Temple - Its Ministry and Service*, chap. 9 "Sabbath in the Temple" (n.p., n.y.) n.p. (accessed on *The Word* Bible Software).
[40] Bacchiocchi, *The Sabbath Under Crossfire*, p. 240.

his way to avoid commenting on vs. 20. Now, can this position stand? Does Romans 14 uphold or abolish the Levitical dietary restrictions? Do the words *koinos* and *akathartos* have different meanings when used in connection with foods or meats? Let us investigate.

We have already explored the reasons why the Mosaic Law is explicitly referred to in Romans 14. Note that Paul deals with the divisive issues of diet and "day" between Romans 13:8 through 15:13. The question is, does a linguistic analysis *prove* that the Mosaic dietary law is at stake? Let's explore the answer.

Writing to a church mixed with Jews and gentiles, Paul says, "One person believes he may eat anything, while the weak person eats only vegetables" (14:2). Right away, both parties should be able to identify themselves and to know who Paul is referring to in either classification. Jewish dietary practices were strictly governed by the Mosaic Law. In Leviticus 11 and Deuteronomy 14, the dietary rules for Israel are clearly laid out. Quite a number of land, sea, and flying animals were "unclean" *to them*. The constant refrain we keep reading in those passages is, "They are unclean to you" (vs. 4-8, 26-28, etc.). The sea creatures that did not match the criteria of having "fins and scales" were "detestable" to them. "Unclean" fowls and insects also fell into this category. (Read the whole passage along with Deut. 14 for the comprehensive category of creatures). Jews were not allowed to eat or touch their carcasses. If they did, they were "unclean until the evening" (vs. 31).[41] If the carcass of an unclean animal touched a vessel or

---

[41] "Unclean" does not mean "unhealthy or unfit for human consumption" as Adventism would want us to believe (see *Seventh-day Adventists Believe*, pp. 318-319, and Bacchiocchi, *The Sabbath in the New Testament*, p. 83.)
Clean, Unclean. The Old Testament, How Uncleanness Was Contracted and Treated- In Old Testament times the ordinary state of most things was "cleanness," but a person or thing could contract ritual "uncleanness" (or "impurity") in a variety of ways: by skin diseases, discharges of bodily fluids, touching something dead (Num. 5:2), or eating unclean foods (Lev. 11; Deut.

an article, it rendered it "unclean" and it had to be either broken or washed (vs. 32-38). Even the carcass of a "clean" animal could render a Jew "unclean" (vs. 39-40). These dietary rules and ritual purity laws *only applied to Jews*. In Deuteronomy 14:21 we read, "You shall not eat anything that has died naturally. You may give it to the sojourner who is within your towns, that he may eat it, or you may sell it to a foreigner. For you are a people holy to the LORD your God...." Did you get that!? Israel could not eat what died naturally, but they could give it to a stranger among them or sell it to a foreigner to make a profit, but they could not eat it.

---

14). An unclean person in general had to avoid that which was holy and take steps to return to a state of cleanness. Uncleanness placed a person in a "dangerous" condition under threat of divine retribution, even death (Lev. 15:31), if the person approached the sanctuary. Uncleanness could lead to expulsion of the land's inhabitants (Lev. 18:25) and its peril lingered upon those who did not undergo purification (Lev. 17:16; Num. 19:12–13). Priests were to avoid becoming ritually defiled (Lev. 21:1–4, 11–12), and if defiled, had to abstain from sacred duties. An unclean layperson could neither eat nor tithe consecrated food (Lev. 7:20–21; Deut. 26:14), had to celebrate the Passover with a month's delay (Num. 9:6–13), and had to stay far away from God's tabernacle (Num. 5:3). Purification varied with the severity of the uncleanness. The most serious to least serious cases in descending order were: skin disease (Lev. 13–14), childbirth (Lev. 12), genital discharges (Lev. 15:3–15, 28–30), the corpse-contaminated priest (Ezek. 44:26–27), the corpse-contaminated Nazirite (Num. 6:9–12), one whose impurity is prolonged (Lev. 5:1–13), the corpse-contaminated layperson (Num. 5:2–4; 19:1–20), the menstruating woman (Lev. 15:19–24), the handling of the ashes of the red cow or the Day of Atonement offerings (Lev. 16:26, 28; Num. 19:7–10), emission of semen (Lev. 15:16–18), contamination by a carcass (Lev. 11:24–40; 22:5), and secondary contamination (Lev. 15; 22:4–7; Num. 19:21–22). Purification always involved waiting a period of time (until evening for minor cases, eighty days for the birth of a daughter), and could also involve ritual washings symbolizing cleansing, atoning sacrifices, and priestly rituals. "Unclean" objects required purification by water (wood, cloth, hide, sackcloth) or fire (metals), or were destroyed (clay pots, ovens), depending on the material (Lev. 11:32–35; Num. 31:21–23). (Walter A. Elwell and Walter A. Elwell, *Evangelical Dictionary of Biblical Theology*, electronic ed., Baker reference library [Grand Rapids: Baker Book House, 1996]).

Notice that this has absolutely nothing to do with health![42] If it had anything to do with health, then we could have charged God with cruelty, favoritism, injustice, and even inhumanity. God instructed Jews to do this because gentiles were not under Torah law nor were they expected to keep them (Psa. 147:19-20; Rom. 2:14; Eph. 2:11-16) unless they converted to Judaism, by undergoing circumcision first (Exo. 12:43-49; Isa. 55:6-7; Eze. 44:6-9; Acts 15:1, 5).[43]

This is one of the main reasons that Jews referred to gentiles as "The Uncircumcised" or "The Uncircumcision" (1 Sam. 17:26; Eph. 2:11; Gal. 2:7; Col. 2:13, etc.,).[44] It is an established, historical fact that Jews were always separated from other nations by four external things—circumcision, diet, the Sabbath, and their dress (Num. 15:37-41). Furthermore, the Jews considered gentiles to be "unclean" (*koinos/akathartos*) and they would not eat nor associate with them (Acts 10:14-15, 28; 11:1-3; Gal. 2:11-13).

---

[42] In the biblical world, health was not seen as a regiment of eating and drinking certain portions of food for particular times per day, abstaining from certain foods and beverages, exercising several times per week, etc. Health was strictly a prerogative of God and was bequeathed to individuals and nations based on covenant faithfulness and obedience (Exo. 15:26; Deut. 28:1-14; Prov. 3:7-8; Isa. 6:10; 58:6-9; Jer. 17:14; Hos. 7:1; etc.).

[43] This rule of being circumcised first *before* one can keep the Law applied to the whole Law, including the Sabbath. Circumcision took precedence over the Sabbath (John 7:21-24). "A non-Jew who observes the Sabbath whilst he is uncircumcised incurs liability for the punishment of death. Why? Because non-Jews were not commanded concerning it.... The Sabbath is a reunion between Israel and God, as it is said, 'It is a sign between Me and the children of Israel' (Exodus 31:17); therefore any non-Jew who, being uncircumcised, thrusts himself between them incurs the penalty of death.... The gentiles have not been commanded to observe the Sabbath." (*Midrash Deuteronomy,* Rabbah 1:21 (Soncino edition, pp. 23-24), as quoted in C. Mervyn Maxwell and P. Gerard Damsteegt, eds., *Source Book for the History of Sabbath and Sunday* (Berrien Springs, Mich.: Seventh-day Adventist Theological Seminary, 1992), 75.)

[44] This was a derisive term and classification for all gentiles.

Simply put, gentiles were "unclean" by virtue of what they ate (in this context), and as a result of their dietary-induced self-contamination, they were seen as "unclean." Jews had to shun associating with them to avoid any form of contamination. Alfred Edersheim gives us a lengthy, but equally powerful, insight into this chasm that existed between Jews and gentiles with regards to diet and other things:

> Readers of the New Testament know what separation Pharisaic Jews made between themselves and heathen. It will be readily understood, that every contact with heathenism and all aid to its rites should have been forbidden, and that in social intercourse any Levitical defilement, arising from the use of what was "common or unclean," was avoided. But Pharisaism went a great deal further than this. Three days before a heathen festival all transactions with gentiles were forbidden, so as to afford them neither direct nor indirect help towards their rites; and this prohibition extended even to private festivities, such as a birthday, the day of return from a journey, etc. On heathen festive occasions a pious Jew should avoid, if possible, passing through a heathen city, certainly all dealings in shops that were festively decorated. It was unlawful for Jewish workmen to assist in anything that might be subservient either to heathen worship or heathen rule, including in the latter the erection of court-houses and similar buildings. It need not be explained to what lengths or into what details Pharisaical punctiliousness carried all these ordinances. From the New Testament we know, that to enter the house of a heathen defiled till the evening (Joh 18:28), and that all familiar intercourse with gentiles forbidden (Act 10:28). So terrible was the intolerance that a Jewess was actually forbidden to give help to her heathen neighbor, when about to become a mother (Avod. S. ii. 1)! It was not a new question to St. Paul, when the Corinthians inquired about the lawfulness of meat sold in the shambles [meat markets] or served up at a feast (1 Cor. 10:25, 1 Cor. 10:27-28). Evidently he had the Rabbinical law on this subject before his mind, while, on the one hand, he avoided the pharisaical bondage of the letter, and, on the other, guarded against either injuring one's own conscience, or offending that of an on-looker. For, according to Rabbi Akiba, "Meat which is about to be brought in heathen worship is lawful, but that which comes out from it is forbidden, because it is like the sacrifices of the dead" (Avod. S. ii.

3). But the separation went much beyond what ordinary minds might be prepared for. Milk drawn from a cow by heathen hands, bread and oil prepared by them, might indeed be sold to strangers, but not used by Israelites. No pious Jew would of course have sat down at the table of a gentile (Act 11:3; Gal 2:12). If a heathen were invited to a Jewish house, he might not be left alone in the room, else every article of food or drink on the table was henceforth to be regarded as unclean. If cooking utensils were bought of them, they had to be purified by fire or by water; knives to be ground anew; spits to be made red-hot before use, etc. It was not lawful to let either house or field, nor to sell cattle, to a heathen; any article, however distantly connected with heathenism, was to be destroyed. Thus, if a weaving shuttle had been made of wood grown in a grove devoted to idols, every web of cloth made by it was to be destroyed; nay, if such pieces had been mixed with others, to the manufacture of which no possible objection could have been taken, these all became unclean, and had to be destroyed. These are only general statements to show the prevalent feeling. It was easy to prove how it pervaded every relationship of life. The heathen, though often tolerant, of course retorted. Circumcision, the Sabbath-rest, the worship of an invisible God, and Jewish abstinence from pork, formed a never-ending theme of merriment to the heathen. Conquerors are not often chary in disguising their contempt for the conquered, especially when the latter presume to look down upon, and to hate them. In view of all this, what an almost incredible truth must it have seemed, when the Lord Jesus Christ proclaimed it among Israel as the object of His coming and kingdom, not to make of the gentile Jews, but of both alike children of one Heavenly Father; not to rivet upon the heathen the yoke of the law, but to deliver from it Jew and gentile, or rather to fulfil its demands for all! The most unexpected and unprepared-for revelation, from the Jewish point of view, was that of the breaking down of the middle wall of partition between Jew and gentile, the taking away of the enmity of the law, and the nailing it to His cross. There was nothing analogous to it; not a hint of it to be found, either in the teaching or the spirit of the times. Quite the opposite. Assuredly, the most unlike thing to Christ were His times; and the greatest wonder of all—"the mystery hidden from ages and generations"—the foundation of one universal Church.[45]

---

[45] Alfred Edersheim, *Sketches of Jewish Social Life*, Chap. 2- Jews and Gentiles in "The Land" (n.p., n.y), n.p. (accessed on *The Word* Bible Software)

So when Paul said in Romans 14:14, "I know and am persuaded in the Lord Jesus that nothing is unclean in itself, but it is unclean for anyone who thinks it unclean," he understood that Jesus had removed the dietary restrictions of the Mosaic Law (Mark 7:14-19); and he himself upholds this and is promoting such a change to foster greater unity between the Jewish and gentile Christians in Rome.

The Greek word for "unclean," used three times in this text (Rom. 14:14), is κοινος (koinos) and Bacchiocchi would have us believe that it is not referring to the Mosaic dietary law, while in fact it does. Here is what *koinos* means and how it is used in the NT:

> κοινός *koinós*; fem. *koiné*, neut. *koinón*, adj. Defiled, common, unclean, to lie common or open to all, common or belonging to several or of which several are partakers (Acts 2:44; 4:32; Titus 1:4; Jude 1:3); unclean hands (Mark 7:2) or meats (Acts 10:14, 28; 11:8; Rom. 14:14; Heb. 10:29, unconsecrated and therefore having no atoning efficacy) such as were common to other nations but were avoided by the Jews as polluted and unclean (Mark 7:2). **Deriv.**: *koinóō* (2840), to make common, unclean; *koinōnós* (2844), an associate, companion, partner, participant. **Syn.**: *akáthartos* (169), unclean; *anósios* (462), unholy, profane. **Ant.**: *katharós* (2513), clean; *hagnós* (53), pure from defilement; *eilikrinḗs* (1506), unalloyed, pure, sincere; *amíantos* (283), undefiled; *ídios* (2398), private.[46]

Did you notice that it is used to refer to "unclean meats" and its synonym is *akathartos*? Very interesting. Here is *akathartos*, what it means and how it is used:

> ἀκάθαρτος *akáthartos*; gen. *akathártou*, masc.–fem., neut. *akátharton*, adj. from the priv. *a* (1), without, and *kathaírō* (2508), to cleanse. Unclean. **(I)** Unclean by legal or ceremonial standards (Acts 10:14, 28; 11:8; Rev. 18:2 [cf. Lev. 5:2; 11:4, 25; 13:45; Deut. 14:7]) whereas in the Sept. it compares with 2 Cor. 6:17 where *akáthartos* seems ultimately to refer to all idolatrous worship and heathen

[46] Spiros Zodhiates, *The Complete Word Study Dictionary: New Testament*, electronic ed. (Chattanooga, TN: AMG Publishers, 2000), κοινος.

impurity. **(II)** Unclean, unfit to be admitted to the peculiar rights and privileges of the church and particularly to baptism (1 Cor. 7:14; Sept.: Is. 52:1; Amos 7:17). **(III)** Unclean by unnatural pollution (Eph. 5:5).

(IV) Unclean as applied to the devils who are frequently called unclean spirits in the NT because, having lost their original purity, they are become unclean themselves and through their solicitations have polluted mankind with all uncleanness and every abomination which the Lord hates (Mark 5:2, 8, 13. See also Matt. 10:1; 12:43; Mark 1:23, 26, 27; 3:11, 30; 6:7; 7:25; 9:25; Luke 4:33, 36; 6:18; 8:29; 9:42; 11:24; Acts 5:16; 8:7; Rev. 16:13). **Deriv.**: *akatharsía* (167), uncleanness. **Syn.**: *bébēlos* (952), profane; *rhuparós* (4508), vile; *ponērós* (4190), evil, but sometimes used as unclean; *koinós* (2839), common, defiled. **Ant.**: *katharós* (2513), clean, pure; *hagnós* (53), pure from defilement; *eilikrinḗs* (1506), sincere, pure; *ámemptos* (273), irreproachable; *gnḗsios* (1103), genuine, true.[47]

If our study were to end right here, the "theological waters" of Romans 14 would already be very clear. However, there is still more evidence to buttress the fact that, indeed, Romans 14 is about the Levitical dietary restrictions and teaches that these dietary restrictions of the Law of Moses have been lifted for Christians. So far, based on the word studies, it is clear that *koinos* and *akathartos* mean essentially the same thing when used in a dietary context. They are synonyms that are used interchangeably.

Another phrase that tells us that the Levitical dietary restrictions are removed in Romans 14 is found in vs. 20 – Gr. "πάντα μὲν καθαρά" (*panta men kathara*- "indeed all foods are clean" [author's translation]). As I had mentioned earlier, it appears that both Bacchiocchi and the *Seventh-day Adventist Bible Commentary* went out of their way to avoid commenting on this phrase because of the proverbial 'rock and a hard place' that they found themselves in theologically and linguistically. Πάντα μὲν καθαρά resonates with the Mosaic Law (LXX/Septuagint), but

---

[47] Zodhiates, *The Complete Word Study Dictionary: New Testament*, electronic ed., ακαθαρτος.

more specifically with the dietary rules of Leviticus 11 and Deuteronomy 14. The noun καθαρά, (neut. plural; καθαρος- masc. singular, καθαρον- neut. singular), is the positive affirmation of what is "clean, pure, and lawful" or permissible to be eaten (LXX Lev. 11:36-37; Deut. 14:11, 20). Ακάθαρτον (neut. singular) is the negation of καθαρον (such is the function of the negating particle alpha "α," equivalent to the English "a" before a noun.) Thus, what is ἀκάθαρτον is "impure, unclean, and unlawful." In the Septuagint, ἀκάθαρτον describes the "unclean food," the person who eats or touches it, the vessel or article that it touches or falls on, etc. (LXX Lev. 11:5-8, 32-36, 39; Deut. 14:7-8, 10-11, etc.). At this juncture, it is important to note that both Jews and gentile Christians who would have read or heard this epistle read could not have misunderstood the thrust of πάντα μὲν καθαρά and its direct reference to Leviticus 11 and Deuteronomy 14, because their text of Scripture was the LXX. J. I. Packer documents:

> Greek was known throughout the Mediterranean regions. In many places, it was more common than Latin, even in a province like Egypt. There were many Jews living outside Jerusalem who did not know Hebrew or could not read it, and for them the Greek translation of the Hebrew Bible (called the Septuagint) was Scripture. The New Testament was written in Greek, and its authors often quote the Septuagint with precision, even in place where the wording of the Septuagint does not agree with the Hebrew text.[48]

Merrill F. Unger corroborates with Packer, "The LXX was the Bible of early Christianity before the NT was written. After the NT Scriptures came on the scene, they were added to the LXX to form

---

[48] J. I. Packer, Merrill Chapin Tenney and William White, Jr., *Nelson's Illustrated Manners and Customs of the Bible* (Nashville, TN: Thomas Nelson, 1997), p. 509.

the completed Scriptures of Christianity."[49] In light of this, there would be no mistaking that the Jews would have understood that Paul was saying that their dietary restrictions and distinctions are now abolished and ought not to be made a point of "quarreling" or controversy with their "strong" gentile brothers. Πάντα μὲν καθαρά also finds strong justification to mean "all (Levitical) foods are clean" by the fact that the phrase is used almost identically elsewhere in the LXX and the NT. In Judges 13, an angel appeared to Manoah's wife with glad tidings that she would have a son. After describing that he will begin to deliver God's people, he further instructed her that he will be a Nazirite and should "...drink no wine or strong drink, and eat nothing unclean..." (Judges 13:7, 14). In the LXX this phrase is rendered as, "...μὴ πίης οἶνον καὶ μέθυσμα καὶ μὴ φάγης πᾶν ἀκάθαρτον...." This is airtight linguistic expression and connection! Πᾶν ἀκάθαρτον, (neut. singular) "eat nothing unclean," is referring to the dietary restrictions of Leviticus 11 and Deuteronomy 14, that Jews were disallowed from eating. Note that it is this very same phrase that we find in the positive affirmation and removal of "clean and unclean" food distinctions in Romans 14:20 "πάντα μὲν καθαρά;" the only difference is that in Judges 13 it is in the negative singular, whereas in Romans 14 it is in the positive plural (The plural versus the singular forms have no bearing on its meaning, as both statements are all-inclusive). We find another repetition of this phrase in the NT that also makes it unmistakable that the dietary laws are removed. In Acts 10, we read of a gentile, God-fearer named Cornelius who had been praying and fasting for four days. During his prayer, an angel appeared to him and instructed him to send for Peter (a Jewish Christian apostle- vs. 1-6). After relating the vision to his servants, he sent them to locate Peter

---

[49] Merrill F. Unger, "Versions of the Scriptures", in *The New Unger's Bible Dictionary*, ed. R. K. Harrison, Rev. and updated ed. (Chicago: Moody Press, 1988).

and to bring him to him. Meanwhile, Peter was hungry; and while the food was being prepared, he went to the housetop to pray, and subsequently had a vision (vs. 9-11). In the vision, he saw a great sheet let down from heaven filled with "all kinds of animals and reptiles and birds of the air," all of which were "unclean" animals based on Peter's response (vs. 12, 14). Then God said to him, "Rise, Peter; kill and eat." But Peter vehemently rejected (three times- vs. 16) with these words, "By no means, Lord; for I have never eaten anything that is common or unclean" (vs. 14). The Greek reads, "Μηδαμῶς, κύριε, ὅτι οὐδέποτε ἔφαγον πᾶν [pan] κοινον [koinon] καὶ ἀκάθαρτον [akatharton]." **This is undeniable Greek linguistics that cannot be circumvented by any honest Bible scholar.**

Πᾶν...ακαθαρτον is the exact phrase that we read in Judges 13:7 and 14, that unmistakably referred to Leviticus 11 and Deuteronomy 14. Here too, in Acts 10:14, it irrefutably refers to the same LXX passages. And this is the same phrase that we read in Romans 14:20, in the positive plural, that removes the Mosaic dietary restrictions. Notice too that in Acts 10:14, both *koinos* and *akathartos* are used together and interchangeably (for intensification), just as they are used in Romans 14:14 and 20. Verse 15 of Acts 10 repeats this same couplet in God's response to Peter, "Ἃ ὁ θεὸς ἐκαθάρισεν σὺ μὴ κοίνου"--"What God has made clean, do not call common."

ἐκαθάρισεν (*ekatharisen*) is the aorist active indicative from καθαριζω (*katharizo*) which is the verb form of καθαρος; and κοίνου (*koinou*) is the present active imperative from κοινοω (*koinoo*) which is also the verb form of *koinos*. What God has declared to be *katharos* should not be called *koinos* or *akathartos* (vs. 14) as Peter did, showing that both words, when referring to the dietary laws of the Old Testament, mean the same thing. While the meaning of the vision primarily focuses on the *koinos* or *akathartos* gentiles, in this case Cornelius, his servants, household, relatives and friends (vs. 17, 24, 28), the vision has a *double meaning and application.* **(1)** The vision primarily refers to the ceremonially unclean foods of the Mosaic Law that were forbidden to be eaten by Jews but permissible for gentiles (as was ably demonstrated). (Remember that it was what the gentiles ate that made them "unclean" and caused that vast chasm between the Jews and themselves.) **(2)** God now having removed the dietary restrictions ("all foods are clean"), the gentiles are no longer to be considered "unclean" by virtue of their diets. And since their food is no longer "unclean" they themselves are not unclean, but are now "clean" brothers with whom Jews can associate and eat with without being contaminated. That is the double meaning and application of the vision.

As a matter of fact, what were "unclean" to the Jews are now considered "clean." This is why Peter was able to eat with Cornelius, his friends, and family (vs. 24, 48; 11:2-3) and all other gentiles (Gal. 2:11-12). Jesus had declared, "All foods clean" (Mark 7:19); and He "has broken down in his flesh the dividing wall of hostility by abolishing the law of commandments expressed in ordinances…" that separate Jews and gentiles (Eph. 2:14-15); and because of that, no one is able to "pass judgment on you in questions of food and drink…." (Col. 2:16). The Kingdom of God, ushered in by our Lord Jesus Christ, "is not a matter of eating and drinking but of righteousness and peace and joy in the Holy Spirit." (Rom. 14:17). Παντα μεν καθαρα—"all foods are clean!"

So now, under the New Covenant, there are no inherently "clean and unclean" foods as was prescribed by the Old Covenant for Jews. All animals are clean and God, through Paul, has given every believer the liberty to personally regard what is clean and what is not clean. Paul also cautions believers to refrain from judging their fellow brothers who have different tastes and convictions about any animal. He says, "I know and am persuaded in the Lord Jesus that nothing is unclean in itself, but it is unclean for anyone who thinks it unclean" (Rom. 14:14). In his letter to Titus, whose church in Crete was being infested with these same Jewish taboos about food promoted by "the circumcision party" (Tit. 1:10, 13), Paul was quick to remind him that, "To the pure, all things are pure, but to the defiled and unbelieving, nothing is pure...." (vs. 15). In the Greek of this text, we find another repetition of πάντα καθαρὰ ("all foods are pure"); further buttressing Paul's conviction about and attitude towards the Mosaic dietary law and the Christian. That is, it is removed and not binding on Christians.

Conclusively, not only is the Mosaic dietary law "at stake" in Romans 14, but it has been *sufficiently* torn down and pulverized.[50] Furthermore, any individual or Church that seeks to enforce dietary restrictions[51] on New Testament believers, the NT

---

[50] First Corinthians 10 provides profound counsels and liberty in eating all meats. Vs. 23 "All things are lawful," but not all things are helpful. "All things are lawful," but not all things build up. 24 Let no one seek his own good, but the good of his neighbor. 25 Eat whatever is sold in the meat market without raising any question on the ground of conscience. 26 For "the earth is the Lord's, and the fullness thereof." 27 If one of the unbelievers invites you to dinner and you are disposed to go, eat whatever is set before you without raising any question on the ground of conscience. 28 But if someone says to you, "This has been offered in sacrifice," then do not eat it, for the sake of the one who informed you, and for the sake of conscience— 29 I do not mean your conscience, but his. For why should my liberty be determined by someone else's conscience? 30 If I partake with thankfulness, why am I denounced because of that for which I give thanks? 31 So, whether you eat or drink, or whatever you do, do all to the glory of God. 32 Give no offense to Jews or to Greeks or to the church of God, 33 just as I try to please everyone in everything I do, not seeking my own advantage, but that of many, that they may be saved.
[51] It is rather interesting that what Scripture says should not be made a requirement for fellowship and a test of salvation (abstinence for certain foods and wine), the Adventist Church makes into both. It requires prospective members to pledge "avoiding the use of that which is harmful, and abstaining

says emphatically that they have departed from the faith and are devoting themselves to teachings and doctrines of demons, and therefore, their teachings should be avoided by believers. I Timothy 4 says, "Now the Spirit expressly says that in later times some will depart from the faith by devoting themselves to deceitful spirits and teachings of demons, through the insincerity of liars whose consciences are seared, who forbid marriage and require abstinence from foods that God created to be received with thanksgiving by those who believe and know the truth. For everything created by God is good, and nothing is to be rejected if it is received with thanksgiving, for it is made holy by the word of God and prayer" (vs. 1-5). Hebrews 13: 9 urges, "Do not be led away by diverse and strange teachings, for it is good for the heart to be strengthened by grace, not by foods, which have not benefited those devoted to them. I Corinthians 8:8 is crystal clear that what we eat or do not eat cannot affect our relationship with God for the better or the worse: "Food will not commend us to God. We are no worse off if we do not eat, and no better off if we do."

---

from all unclean foods; from the use, manufacture, or sale of alcoholic beverages…" before they are baptized and accepted into membership. (*Seventh-day Adventist Church Manual*, p. 46). Ellen White goes so far as to state that, "Tea and coffee drinking is a sin…" and advised Adventists, "In relation to tea, coffee, tobacco, and alcoholic drinks, the only safe course is to touch not, taste not, handle not." (*Counsels on Diet and Foods*, p. 425, par.3, and p. 430, par.1). This diametrically opposes the counsel of Scripture in Romans 14 and Colossians 2:16-23.

CHAPTER THREE

ROMANS 14:5-6- THE SABBATH OR "FAST DAYS"

(A) The "day" is not a reference to "days of fasting."

Bacchiocchi contended that the "day" referred to in Romans 14:5-6 is not the Sabbath but rather "day of fasting" that believers regarded with differing opinions. He buttressed his position by referring to chapter 8 of *The Didache,* in which Christians were instructed to "fast" on Wednesday and Friday to differentiate themselves from Jews who fasted on Tuesday and Thursday. As we examine the evidence, we will notice that there was *never* a controversy in the Gospels nor in the early church about days of fasting. Neither can that reference in *The Didache* be interpolated into Romans 14. Therefore, Romans 14 cannot be speaking about fasting, demonstrating that the Sabbath is in view.

In the New Testament, we find various references to fasting. There are three related Greek words that are used to refer to fasting: **(1)** νηστις *(nestis)* –n. fasting, not having eaten (used 2 times in the NT- Matt. 15:32; Mark 8:3) **(2)** νηστεια *(nesteia)* - n. a) a fasting, fast (voluntary, as a religious exercise, whether private or public) b) fasting caused by need or poverty (used 8 times in the NT- Matt. 17:21; Mark 9:29; Acts 14:23; Luke 2:37; Acts 27:9; 1 Cor. 7:5; 2 Cor. 6:6; and 11:27), and **(3)** νηστευω *(nesteuo)* – verb - to abstain from food and drink (as a religious exercise) (used 22 times in the NT- Matt. 4:2; 6:16-18; Mark 2:18, etc.,).

It is critical to note that of the number of times that fasting is referred to in the New Testament, days of fasting were never even discussed nor were there ever a controversy about them.

Jesus fasted during His lifetime and ministry but a specific day was not an issue (Matt. 4:2; Mark 1:35; John 4:31-34, etc.). He took it for granted that fasting would have continued during His ministry

(Matt. 6:16-18). He taught this not as an obligation for Christians to fast but that doing so is congruous with prayer (Matt. 6:5-15) and humility (Matt. 6:19-34). Despite this, He never enjoined a specific day. In Matthew 9:14-17, John's disciples questioned Jesus why were they and the Pharisees fasting often but His disciples neglected to do so, to which Jesus responded that it was not necessary while He was with His disciples (cf. Mark 2:18-22; Luke 5:33-35). The controversy that John's disciples raised was not regarding the day or time of fasting but the act of fasting itself.

In Luke 2:37, we see the description of the widowed prophetess Anna as continually, "worshiping with fasting and prayer night and day," merely highlighting her continuous, pious habit and lifestyle but not enforcing a time of fasting. In Luke 18:12, Jesus taught the people an important spiritual lesson in the parable about a Pharisee who fasted "twice a week" and thought that he was better than the tax collector. This was not a recommendation to fast on specific days, "twice a week." This was merely a parable that Jesus used to illustrate a point—that it is futile to be self-righteous and to trust in one's righteousness, while despising others who appear less righteous and religious. Acts 10:30 reveals that the gentile Cornelius, fasted for four days. Again, this is a descriptive statement and does not represent a recommendation in regard to when and how long to fast. In speaking of fasting and prayer, Acts 13:1-3 speaks of the activities of the prophets and disciples in that regard. There is no recommendation nor controversy in regard to days of fasting (cf. 14:23).

Acts 27:9's mention of "the Fast" is a reference to the Day of Atonement which occurred about the end of September, after which navigation was considered dangerous until mid-March. Robert Jamieson comments on this verse, "**was now dangerous, because the fast was now … past**—that of the day of atonement, answering to the end of *September* and beginning of *October,* about which time the navigation is pronounced unsafe by writers of authority."[52] Because Jews had to fast on that day (in Lev. 16:31; 23:27, 29, "afflict yourselves" means "to fast"), "the Fast" became one of its standard names and references. In 1 Corinthians 7:5, Paul speaks of the purpose for which married couples should abstain from sexual activities, prayer and fasting (KJV), but he does not enjoin a specific day of fasting nor is a controversy hinted there. The last two references to fasting (νηστεια) in the NT merely state facts about Paul's enduring hunger (fasting) and privation (2 Cor.6:5; 11:27) during his missionary journeys. Having looked at these major references to fasting (*nesteia/nesteuo*) in the NT, it is obvious to see that days of fasting were never recommended nor was there ever a controversy regarding them.

Instantly, we can detect that Bacchiocchi's conclusion is not obtainable from the evidences adduced from the NT. As a matter of fact, the respective Greek words for fasting in the NT (νηστις, νηστεια, and νηστευω) are *never even used* in the Book of Romans, nor is fasting ever discussed in the same, and the idea of fasting is remotely foreign to the context of chapter 14.

As part of his polemic, Bacchiocchi elicited 'evidence' from *The Didache* to sustain his position that Romans 14 is a reference to "fast days." He stated:

> The preference over days in Romans presumably had to do with fast-days rather than feast-days, since the context deals with abstinence from meat and wine (Rom 14:2, 6, 21). Support for this view is provided by the *Didache* (Ch. 8) which enjoins Christians to fast on

---

[52] Robert Jamieson, A. R. Fausset and David Brown, *Commentary Critical and Explanatory on the Whole Bible* (Oak Harbor, WA: Logos Research Systems, Inc., 1997), Ac 27:9–10.

Wednesday and Friday rather than on Monday and Thursday like the Jews.[53]

The Didache does state, "But as for your fasts, let them not be with the hypocrites, for they fast on the second and fifth days of the week, but do ye fast on the fourth and sixth days."[54] At first glance, it appears that this analysis and conclusion is accurate because, indeed, a controversy did occur between Jews and Christians with regards to fast days. But upon analyzing the dating of Romans and *The Didache*, it becomes clear that the "day" of Romans 14 and the "fast days" of *The Didache* are anachronistic and unrelated. Therefore, the statement from *The Didache* cannot be read into Romans 14. James P. Sweeney posits that the Book of Romans was written around A.D. 54-56.[55] While James Dunn gives a more comprehensive view:

> Besides this question of the setting of the letter within the life and work of Paul, the more detailed questions of precise *date* and place of *origin* are of comparatively less importance, since little hangs on them for purposes of exegesis, except insofar as they illuminate the background of certain passages, particularly 13:6–7 and 14:1 ff. Suffice it to say that the letter must have been written sometime in the 50's A.D., probably in the middle 50's, and most probably late 55/early 56, or late 56/early 57.[56]

Dunn's dating for the writing of the Book of Romans is accepted by the majority of NT scholars. We can conclusively say that Romans is a pre-A.D. 60's book of the NT. This piece of information

---

[48] Bacchiocchi, *The Sabbath in the New Testament*, p. 84.

[54] *Didache* 8:1, Translated by Charles H. Hoole.

[55] James P. Sweeney, "Chronology of the New Testament", in *The Lexham Bible Dictionary*, ed. John D. Barry, David Bomar, Derek R. Brown et al. (Bellingham, WA: Lexham Press, 2016).

[56] James D. G. Dunn, vol. 38A, *Romans 1–8*, *Word Biblical Commentary* (Dallas: Word, Incorporated, 1998), p. 43. (emphases in original)

might seem unimportant but given the subject under discussion, it is of tantamount importance. *The Didache* has a much later dating. Henry Cowan comments concerning *The Didache*, "Probably the document went through a series of recensions and the date or dates of composition may be put between 80 and 120 A.D."[57] Robert A. Kraft adds:

> Some commentators argue for a date of effective origin as early as around 70 or soon thereafter (Kleist 1948; Rordorf and Tuilier 1978), and others as late as the later 2nd century (Vokes, 1970) or even the 3rd century (Peterson, 1959). The fact that Christian witnesses from the 4th century onward, especially in the vicinity of Egypt, provide the strongest evidence for the existence of *The Didache* tradition, is the necessary starting point for controlled discussions of its origin and date.[58]

Based on these two statements and the strong evidences referred to by Kraft, *The Didache* has to be placed at late 1st Century A.D. to early 2nd century or after. And even if it is dated in the 70's, that is still telling evidence.

Now, what do these dates reveal to us with regards to the subject under discussion? A simple but profound truth, and that is, the reference to "day" in Romans 14:5-6, is not the same "fast days" that are referenced in *The Didache*. Romans predates *The Didache* by a *comfortable two or more decades.* This simple fact means that the later development among Jews and Christians, with regards to days of fasting in *The Didache*, is not what is being spoken about in Romans 14. It is scholarly irresponsible to read the statement of *The Didache* into Romans 14, as that situation is remote to the author and succeeds him by two or more decades. **Simply put, Paul could not have written so emphatically,**

---

[57] Henry Cowan, "Literature, Sub-Apostolic", in *The International Standard Bible Encyclopaedia, Volumes 1–5*, ed. James Orr, John L. Nuelsen, Edgar Y. Mullins and Morris O. Evans (Chicago: The Howard-Severance Company, 1915), p. 1898.

[58] Robert A. Kraft, "Didache" in vol. 2, *The Anchor Yale Bible Dictionary*, ed. David Noel Freedman (New York: Doubleday, 1992), p. 197.

hortatively, and conclusively about a "fast day" issue that was nonexistent in his time. If the statement of Romans 14:5-6 was made in the Gospel of John or in the Book of Revelation (both believed to have been written in the late 1st century A.D.), then the chances would have been high that "days of fasting" is what is being referenced, but for the book of Romans it is highly unlikely, *historically and chronologically*. With this in mind, either Dr. Bacchiocchi was scholarly irresponsible or he was tergiversate, in his conclusion, in order to evade the obvious—that observing the Sabbath and the Jewish feast days is not essential to salvation, they are matters of *personal conviction,* and that opinions regarding them should not *create division* within the Body of Christ. But given the official position of his Church and prophetess,[59] it is not difficult to understand why Bacchiocchi

---

[59] The SDA Church sees the Sabbath as binding on all people and they are required to observe it. It sees it as a symbol of "redemption in Christ," a "sign of sanctification, a token of allegiance," and "God's perpetual sign of His eternal covenant."(These descriptions of and beliefs about the Sabbath are in conflict with the NT, as the NT describes the Holy Spirit in such terms [Rom. 8:9, 14-16; 2 Cor. 1:21-22; Eph. 1:13-14; 4:30; 1 Pet. 1:2, etc.]). Adventists also believe that the Sabbath will play a *critical and decisive role* in the salvation of all humanity before the "Second Advent" when "the whole world" will be thrown into a conflict where "the central issue will be obedience to God's law and the observance of the Sabbath." And those who "reject it will eventually receive the mark of the beast." (*Seventh-day Adventists Believe*, pp. 281, 295-296)

The prophetess of the Adventist Church, Ellen G. White, says these things concerning the Sabbath and its relation to a believer's salvation: "It means eternal salvation to keep the Sabbath holy unto the Lord. God says: "Them that honor Me I will honor." 1 Samuel 2:30." (*Counsels for the Church*, p. 264, par. 4).

"The seal of the living God is placed upon those who conscientiously keep the Sabbath of the Lord."—*Seventh-day Adventist Bible Commentary*, vol. 7, p. 980 (1897).

"Those who would have the seal of God in their foreheads must keep the Sabbath of the fourth commandment."— (*Last Day Events*, p. 220, par. 2).

could not have accepted what Romans 14:5-6 clearly says, so he

---

"True observance of the Sabbath is the sign of loyalty to God."— (Ibid, p. 220, par. 3)

"The observance of the Lord's memorial, the Sabbath instituted in Eden, the seventh-day Sabbath, is the test of our loyalty to God."—Letter 94, 1900. (*Last Day Events*, p. 220, par. 5)

"I saw that the present test on the Sabbath could not come until the mediation of Jesus in the holy place was finished and He had passed within the second veil; therefore Christians who fell asleep before the door was opened into the most holy, when the midnight cry was finished, at the seventh month, 1844, and who had not kept the true Sabbath, now rest in hope, for they had not the light and the test on the Sabbath which we now have since that door was opened. I saw that Satan was tempting some of God's people on this point. Because so many good Christians have fallen asleep in the triumphs of faith and have not kept the true Sabbath, they were doubting about its being a test for us now. . . ." (Ibid, p. 222, par. 2)

"The sign, or seal, of God is revealed in the observance of the seventh-day Sabbath, the Lord's memorial of creation. . . . The mark of the beast is the opposite of this—the observance of the first day of the week."—*Testimonies for the Church*, vol. 8, p. 117 (1904).

"God has given men the Sabbath as a sign between Him and them as a test of their loyalty. Those who, after the light regarding God's law comes to them, continue to disobey and exalt human laws above the law of God in the great crisis before us, will receive the mark of the beast."—*Evangelism*, p. 235 (1900).

"The Sabbath will be the great test of loyalty, for it is the point of truth especially controverted. When the final test shall be brought to bear upon men, then the line of distinction will be drawn between those who serve God and those who serve Him not." (*Last Day Events*, p. 225, par. 2)

"The Sabbath is the great test question. It is the line of demarcation between the loyal and true and the disloyal and transgressor. This Sabbath God has enjoined, and those who claim to be commandment keepers, who believe that they are now under the proclamation of the third angel's message, will see the important part the Sabbath of the fourth commandment holds in that message. It is the seal of the living God. They will not lessen the claims of the Sabbath to suit their business of convenience."—Manuscript 34, 1897. (*3 Selected Messages*, p. 423, par. 2)

"I saw that the holy Sabbath is, and will be, the separating wall between the true Israel of God and unbelievers; and that the Sabbath is the great question to unite the hearts of God's dear, waiting saints." (*Early Writings*, p. 33, par. 1)

appears to resort to purposeful obfuscation. Based on these facts, I *resolutely conclude* that the "day" in Romans 14 cannot be a reference to differences of "fast days" among Jewish and gentile Christians in Rome as referenced in *The Didache*. The issue with "fast days" in *The Didache* developed decades later in the Christian Church and may not have even existed in Rome, even when it became an issue.

(B) The "Weak", the "strong," and the Sabbath in Romans 14:5-6.

Bacchiocchi states concerning the weak and the strong believer in Romans 14:

> Finally, if as generally presumed, it was the "weak" believer who observed the Sabbath, Paul would classify himself with the "weak" since he observed the Sabbath and other Jewish feasts (Acts 18:4, 19; 17:1, 10, 17; 20:16). Paul, however, views himself as "strong" ("we who are strong"—Rom. 15:1); thus, he could not have been thinking of Sabbath-keeping when he speaks of the preference over days.[60]

At first glance, this appears to be a strong argument by Dr. Bacchiocchi, but upon examining Paul's Sabbath activities in the Book of Acts, one can readily observe two things: **(1)** one would never see any verifiable instruction to keep the Sabbath in the accounts given of Paul's activities nor that Paul's activities were considered to be Sabbath-keeping. For example, we do not read, in Acts 17:2, anything like, "And Paul went in, as was his custom, and on three Sabbath days *to keep the Sabbath*." Such a notion is non-existent in the Book of Acts. **(2)** All of the accounts of Paul's Sabbath activities in Acts are *descriptive and missional*—not *prescriptive and exemplary*. A very casual reading of Paul's

---

[60] Bacchiocchi, *The Sabbath Under Crossfire*, p. 241.

Sabbath activities reveals that every city or town he went to, he first sought to preach the Gospel of Christ to his Jewish brethren (Acts 13:14-15, 42-46; 17:1-5; 18:1-4), and as can be observed, in all of these instances the majority of them always rejected his message and persecuted him. As a matter of fact, Acts 18 is the last account of any of Paul's Sabbath missional activities to the Jews. After they rejected his preaching about Jesus Christ, the Messiah, Paul "shook out his garments" (cf. Matt. 10:14; Neh. 5:13), pronounced their guilt upon them, and informed them that their actions represented rebellion that would bring retribution on them that will result in their doom. He told them, "Your blood be on your own heads" (cf. 2 Sam. 1:16; Eze. 33:4, 9; Matt. 27:25): and then he directed his ministry to the gentiles (Acts 18:5-7). This incident marked the second time that Paul had to do this to the Jews, as he had done so before in Antioch for the same reason (Acts 13:46, 50-51).

Bacchiocchi, again the victim of his own circular reasoning that Paul could not possibly be referring to the Sabbath, concludes that Paul would not consider Sabbath-keepers as "weak" when he himself "kept" the Sabbath and classified himself with the "strong."

For Paul to consider Sabbath-keepers "weak" while he classified himself "strong" is not incongruous when one understands that Paul was not keeping the Sabbath simply because he visited Jewish synagogues on the Sabbath. He was there to reason with the Jews about Christ being the Messiah in an effort to get them to accept Jesus Christ as their Lord and Savior. When he was with the Jews, he would do Jewish things. He visited Jewish synagogues on the Sabbath to preach the Gospel to them because he knew that's when they would be gathered together. The same way that a former Muslim, converted to Christianity, would visit mosques on Fridays, at the peril of his life, to preach Christ to his brethren. This person's actions cannot be equated with "keeping Friday."

His visit to the mosque would be missional by intent. Paul explained his own adaptable ways as the means by which he could encounter various people groups to preach the Gospel in order to "save some." In one instance Paul actually stated that he would become "weak" in order to reach weak people such as were some of the Corinthians. In 1 Corinthians 9:19-23 we read:

> For though I am free from all, I have made myself a servant to all, that I might win more of them. To the Jews I became as a Jew, in order to win Jews. To those under the law I became as one under the law (though not being myself under the law) that I might win those under the law. To those outside the law I became as one outside the law (not being outside the law of God but under the law of Christ) that I might win those outside the law. To the weak I became weak, that I might win the weak. I have become all things to all people, that by all means I might save some. I do it all for the sake of the gospel, that I may share with them in its blessings.

Paul considered himself "strong," but he would have identified with the "weak" in order to save them. In his longing desire to save his fellow Israelites (Rom. 10:1), he even expressed a willingness to become "accursed" and "cut off" from Christ for their sake! We read in Romans 9:3-5:

> For I could wish that I myself were accursed and cut off from Christ for the sake of my brothers, my kinsmen according to the flesh. 4 They are Israelites, and to them belong the adoption, the glory, the covenants, the giving of the law, the worship, and the promises. 5 To them belong the patriarchs, and from their race, according to the flesh, is the Christ, who is God over all, blessed forever. Amen.

Given this understanding, it is not at all a farfetched idea that the preferred "day" in Romans 14 was the Sabbath that was kept by "weak" Jewish Christian believers. However, Paul is not saying that Sabbath-keeping is for "weak believers."

Seeing that Bacchiocchi started off with the wrong proposition, let us re-examine what Paul is saying in order to get it right. It is not that Paul considers Sabbath-keeping for weak believers. Paul's issue is with those who are "weak *in faith*" (14:1) and feel it is necessary to supplement their faith in Christ *with* the dietary rules of the Old Testament, the Sabbath, and other appointed festivals, while passing judgment on those who differ. Dunn gives a great examination here:

> "We, the strong," does not appear till 15:1, but it is already evident in the very use of the phrase that Paul numbers himself with "the strong" (14:14, 20). It is not that Paul regards "weakness" per se as something defective (though cf. 5:6). On the contrary, he elsewhere regards human or physical weakness as the very locus of divine power in this present epoch (particularly 2 Cor. 4:7–11; 11:30; 12:5, 9–10; 13:4, 9). What is defective here is the faith—"weak *in faith*." What he means by that is already clear from 4:19: to be "weak in faith" is to fail to trust God completely and without qualification…. In this case the weakness is trust in God *plus* dietary and festival laws, trust in God *dependent* on observance of such practices, a trust in God which leans on the crutches of particular customs and not on God alone, as though they were an integral part of that trust.[61]

The "weak in faith" in Romans 14 are clearly the Jewish Christians. Their faith had not matured, like Paul's, to understand that those issues were mere shadows (Col. 2:16-17) that are not essential in Christ and the New Covenant faith, and that their observance is now optional. In this regard, gentiles exhibited a "stronger" faith in Christ because those things were never obstacles for them; whereas for the Jews, the Law caused them to have a "weaker" faith. Christ once contrasted a gentile centurion's "strong" faith with the "weak" one of Israelites when He said, "I tell you, not even in Israel have I found such faith." (Luke 7:9). Paul had expounded on this dichotomy earlier when he said:

> What shall we say, then? That Gentiles who did not pursue righteousness have attained it, that is, a righteousness that is by faith;

---

[61] James D. G. Dunn, vol. 38B, *Romans 9–16*, Word Biblical Commentary (Dallas: Word, Incorporated, 1998), pp. 797-798.

31 but that Israel who pursued a law that would lead to righteousness did not succeed in reaching that law. 32 Why? Because they did not pursue it by faith, but as if it were based on works. They have stumbled over the stumbling stone, 33 as it is written, "Behold, I am laying in Zion a stone of stumbling, and a rock of offense...." (Rom. 9:30-33).

This weakness "in faith" may explain why Paul took a softer approach with the Jewish Christians in Rome on the matters of diet and days, whereas he took a much stronger approach with the Galatians and Colossians on the same issues (Gal. 2:11-21; 3:1-5; 4:8-11; 5:4; Col. 2:11-23). Paul's approach in Romans seems to be softer because the differences between Jews and gentiles on these matters were mere "opinions" on which they "judged" and "despised" each other, without compromising faith in Christ and the Gospel. By contrast, in Galatia and Colossae the focus on diet and days was outright heresy that compromised both faith in Christ and the Gospel, making diet and observance of "days" *requisites for* salvation. Dale Ratzlaff makes the same observation when he said:

> If, indeed, this passage does refer to Sabbath days then Paul simply says "let each man be fully convinced in his own mind" (v.5). This is a much softer answer than he gave to the Colossians and Galatians. And we can see why. There were many Jewish Christians in the Roman church to which Paul was writing who may have still been keeping *many* of the old covenant regulations. It is of utmost importance to note the difference between the situation mentioned in Rome and that of Galatia. In Galatia the false teachers were saying that one *must* observe the old covenant rituals for salvation, thus compromising the Gospel. In Rome, however, some believers were passing judgment on each other's "opinions" regarding a number of issues including the observance of "days." The problem in Rome, then, was not a compromise of the gospel; rather it was diversity of opinions that caused disunity within the church.[62]

---

[62] Dale Ratzlaff, *Sabbath in Christ* (Glendale, AZ: LAM Publications, LLC, 2010),

Given this examination, I conclude that the believer in Romans 14 who is "weak in faith" and "esteems one day as better than another" is the Jewish Christian. On the other hand, the "strong" believer who "eats all things" and "esteems all days alike" is the gentile Christian. Paul is in no way suggesting that Sabbath-keeping is for the "weak" believer— rather, the "weak in faith" had scruples about Sabbath-keeping, believed that he should observe it, and judged his "strong" brother who did not. I have many "strong" Christian friends who are Sabbatarians and also vegetarians. I also know of many Sabbatarian churches that maintain the Levitical dietary distinctions and abstain from certain foods. The difference with them is that they know and understand that these matters are not mandatory for salvation, and also neither do they contend with or condemn other Christians who differ over such matters. In sharp contrast, Adventism and its prophetess, Ellen G. White, make them both *salvific and mandatory* (as was shown), and are also engaged in a self-generated and self-sustained theological war with Christians over such matters. Ellen White goes so far as to state that "...the rejection of God's holy memorial [the Sabbath] will decide the fate of many professing Christians."[63] This statement is clearly contradictory to the teachings of the New Testament and elevates the Sabbath to a critical salvation issue. Dr. Jerry Gladson commented on this unfortunate focus of Adventist Sabbatarianism in these words:

> The Sabbath, for practical purposes, is the *sine qua non* of the denomination, its principal teaching. Adventists make more far-reaching claims about the Sabbath than any other seventh-day Sabbatarian group. They believe which day Christians observe— Saturday or Sunday—will eventually become the final, decisive test for the entire world, cutting across all other lines of religious distinction.

---

p. 183. (Emphasis in the original)
[63] White, *Review and Herald*, Dec. 20, 1898.

The Sabbath isn't merely one option among several.[64]

This stance of the Adventist Church is unbiblical and appears to represent a heretical point of view. The "strong" gentile, on the other hand, who "esteems all days alike" appears to have "despised" his brother because of such scruples. Paul's conclusion in regards to this "day" issue is, "Each one should be fully convinced in his own mind" (vs. 5) and that they should "pursue what makes for peace and for mutual up-building" (vs. 19), as they keep "walking in love" (vs. 15).

Even though Bacchiocchi did not use this argument, it is worth mentioning that some Sabbatarians, especially Adventists, Armstrongites, and Hebrew Roots Movement "Christians," believe that since Romans 14:5-6 does not use the customary Greek word σαββατον (*sabbaton*) in referring to the "day," it is proof that Romans 14 is not talking about the Sabbath. They also contend that adjectives such as "holy," "sacred," "worship," etc., are not used in describing this day that is esteemed above others. These objections ignore an underlying set of factors that indicate otherwise. Terrence O'Hare makes this observation about Romans 14:5-6:

> It must be remembered that the Sabbath was more important than any other Jewish holy day and venerated for its special holiness and elevated status. If there was a day to esteem, a day that required keeping, then the Sabbath is it. In all likelihood, Paul wrote to those Jews who continued to meet on feast days and the Sabbath.[65]

With this in mind, one cannot rule out that the Sabbath was not first and foremost in Paul's mind when he penned these words,

[64] Jerry Gladson, *A Theologian's Journey from Seventh-day Adventism to Mainstream Christianity* (Glendale, AZ: LAM Publications, LLC, 2000), p. 321. (emphasis in original)

[65] Terrence D. O'Hare, *The Sabbath Complete and the Ascendancy of First-Day Worship* (Eugene, OR: Wipf and Stock Publishers, 2011), p. 196.

"One person esteems one day as better than another, while another esteems all days alike. Each one should be fully convinced in his own mind. The one who observes the day, observes it in honor of the Lord...." (Rom. 14:5-6). Neither can one rule out that, given the conviction of his Jewish audience, they would not have understood this to be referring to their "venerated and elevated" Sabbath. So, the absence of σαββατον and adjectives that are often used to refer to the weekly Sabbath do not remove the nearly overwhelming evidence that the Sabbath is referred to here. After surveying the "fast days" versus "holy days" of scholarly opinion in regard to this passage, D. R. de Lacey concluded, "The balance of probability, then, is in favor of the Sabbath being included in the "days" of Romans 14:5. Paul allows that the keeping of such days is purely a matter of individual conscience."[66] It is worth repeating that the Sabbath has to be in view because it was 'esteemed' above other days by the Jews, because it was to be "observed" (Exo. 20:8-11; Deut. 5:15), and because it certainly was a "day" (Lev. 23:3).

Analyzing few points from the Greek sentence also lends support to this understanding and conclusion. The first part of Romans 14:5 reads, "Ὅς μὲν κρίνει ἡμέραν παρ' ἡμέραν, ὃς δὲ κρίνει πᾶσαν ἡμέραν...." The anarthrous (indefinite) noun ἡμέραν ("day") refers to any day that was esteemed or could be esteemed against another day. Surely the Sabbath fits into this category as it was set against and esteemed above other days. In the second clause, the adjective "all" (πασαν) that modifies the noun "day" (ἡμέραν) is contextually all inclusive. The definition of this word includes, without exception, <u>all</u> of whatever it is that it is being modified. For example, *all* the boys 2 years old and

---

[66] D. R. de Lacey, "The Sabbath/Sunday Question and the Law in the Pauline Corpus" in *From Sabbath to Lord's Day: A Biblical, Historical, and Theological Investigation*, edited by D. A. Carson (previously published by Zondervan, 1982), reprinted (Eugene, Oregon: Wipf and Stock Publishers, 1999), p. 182.

younger in Bethlehem were killed by Herod (Matt. 2:16): *all* who are weary and burdened can come to Jesus for rest (Matt. 11:28). Jesus will come with *all* of His holy angels (Matt. 25:31). Jesus possesses *all* power in heaven and earth (Matt. 28:18): *all* nations should be evangelized with the Gospel (vs. 19): *all* who believe in Jesus will not perish but have eternal life (John 3:16). Jesus' name is above *all* names (Phil. 2:9). The redeemed people of God will be from *all* nations, tribes, peoples, and languages (Rev. 7:9). God will make *all* things new at the end of time (Rev. 21:5), etc. So the "all days" of Romans 14:5 that are esteemed alike include feast days, fast days, the Sabbath day, birthdays, national holidays, "pagan" days, etc. As long as it is a "day," it is included in the category of "all days." So, the Sabbath fits into both categories whether to be regarded as "better" than other days or to be regarded as "all days." And the powerful and unequivocal injunction that Paul gives to either party that holds either conviction is, "Each one should be fully convinced in his own mind." Paul was a scholar par excellence (Gal. 1:14; 2 Pet. 3:15-16). He knew the thrusts and nuances of the Greek language, and he most certainly knew how this statement would have been understood by his learned audience. But yet, he was forthright in his exhortation and conclusion. It is profound to note too that Paul does not condemn the one who regards all days alike, knowing that the Sabbath would be included, neither does he urge such a one to "straighten up" and regard the Sabbath as above other days. Instead, he maintains that the observing of days is a personal matter that is done in "honour of the Lord." (vs. 6). Therefore, the one who observes the Sabbath or any particular day, does so in "honour of the Lord." And the one who observes "all days alike"-- that is, he or she has no conviction to keep the Sabbath or any other day (as they are regarded with the same degree in his mind)-- also does so in "honour of the Lord."

Furthermore, it has been sufficiently demonstrated that the

Mosaic Law is being discussed in this passage (13:8-15:13) and that love fulfils *all* of it. That is, loving one's neighbor as one's self fulfils the *requirements and demands* of the Mosaic Law, including the minute particulars of Sabbath observance (13:8-10); and having made this clear, Paul highlights two issues of the Mosaic Law that constantly evoked quarrels among Jews and gentiles—diet and the Sabbath—and exhorted them to be tolerant and non-judgmental. Consequently then, despite the absence of σαββατον and other adjectives that customarily described the Sabbath in the OT, it is still obvious to see that no matter from which angle we examine this pericope, all roads still lead to the Sabbath in vs. 5-6.[67] The big question that should be asked now is, why would Paul consider the Sabbath to be a matter of "personal conviction?" We will now explore that answer.

---

[67] Paul does not need to refer to "worship" in Romans 14, as he is writing to a mixed congregation of Jews and gentiles who naturally "worshiped" together and who would have heard this epistle read together. The use of adjectives such as "holy," "sacred," etc., is not necessary in vs. 5-6 to describe the "day" that is regarded above other days. Those adjectives are never used elsewhere with the Sabbath in the New Testament, yet we all, including Sabbatarians, understand that the Sabbath is being discussed when it is either mentioned or referred to, whether directly or indirectly.

CHAPTER FOUR

WHY IS SABBATH-KEEPING A MATTER OF PERSONAL CONVICTION IN ROMANS 14?

(A) It is a shadow of Christ and a symbol of Redemption.

In the most explicit way, Paul calls the Sabbath (along with the other festivals of Israel) a "shadow" that has Christ as its Substance (Col. 2:16-17). The Greek word σκια (skia),[68] for "shadow" in Colossians 2:17, means "a shade, an image cast by an object and representing the form of that object, an adumbration." A shadow faintly represents or points to the "body/image." A shadow can never be the reality itself or provide shadow for its own shadow. Rather, a shadow provides only a rough, undefined outline of a real object that is markedly void of detail. Since Paul calls the Sabbath a "shadow," we should not expect it to continue to have its full force and meaning when the Reality has arrived. The Old Testament, instead of calling the Sabbath a shadow, designates it as the specific "sign" of the Mosaic Covenant (Exo. 31:12-17; Eze. 20:12, 20). Terrence O'Hare provides a wonderful definition of and insights to "signs:"

> The word "sign" is translated from derivatives of the Hebrew (*owth*) and Greek (*semeion*) and has a semantic range of meanings: "mark," "miracle," "prophecy," "token," "evidence," and "monument." In Genesis, the mark for Cain was a reminder to him and others of God's gracious protection of his life even though he murdered his brother Abel (Gen. 4:16). The rainbow was a sign to Noah and continues to be a sign to successive generations of God's promise not to flood the earth again (Gen. 9:16-17). Circumcision was a sign to Abraham of his covenant with the Lord (Gen. 17:11). The exodus and journey to Mount Sinai were a sign to the Israelites that Moses was indeed sent

---

[68] This word, "skia", is used 7 times in the NT where it describes 1) the shadow of death (Matt. 4:16; Luke 1:79), 2) the shadow of a tree and a person (Mark 4:32; Acts 5:15), 3) the Mosaic Law and its services (Heb. 8:5; 10:1) and 4) the food and drink laws and festivals of Israel (Col. 2:16-17).

by the Lord (Ex. 3:12). The blood on the door posts was a sign to God where the believing families were residing (Ex.12:13). The Feast of Unleavened Bread (Ex. 13:9), the law of the Firstborn (Ex. 13:16), and the Sabbath (Ex. 31:13, 17) were all signs of God's power to redeem Israel from Egypt. A sign established or identified by God is usually a visual or tangible reminder or representation of a historical experience in order to stir up action, belief, or caution. Signs communicate ideas associated with the sign and demand a response (Ex. 4:8-9). In other words, a sign takes second place to the idea or the event that it signifies or represents. Notwithstanding Jesus' apparent denigration of signs to the Pharisees, He essentially identified Himself as the fulfilment of the signs of Scripture. He fulfilled the sign of Jonah, not only in His preaching repentance to Israel (Luke 11:29-30), but in His forthcoming resurrection and preaching the Kingdom of God to the gentiles due to widespread Jewish unbelief (Matt. 12:39-41). It is well-known that signs of the Old Covenant "had respect to and shadowed forth Christ who was to come," and "were to continue until the time of reformation or the Advent of Christ," but New Covenant signs "regard Christ as having come," and "continue until the end of the world." The Sabbath was a sign of the Old Covenant (Ex. 31:13, 17) that shadowed forth the glorious redemption in Jesus Christ and, having fulfilled that purpose, is no longer binding in any of its exterior rites. What are the external and visible signs of Sabbath-keeping? The weekly physical rest signified the believers complete trust in His perfect redemption. The prohibition from work signifies that it is the Lord's work in our redemption and not our own. The restraint from business signifies that His redemption cannot be bought or sold like merchandise. Abiding and no cooking signify that our redemption is a restoration of the original garden paradise. The Lord identified the Sabbath as a sign and it is defined rites performed upon that day. As a sign of the Old Covenant, the Sabbath "had respect to and shadowed forth Christ" and is no longer pertinent as a sign under the New Covenant. The sun went down on the Sabbath, but we have in this new day the Lord Jesus Christ, the Person to whom pointed the Sabbath signs.[69]

Already, we can begin to peer into the mind of Paul and also the

---

[69] O'Hare, *The Sabbath Complete and the Ascendancy of First-Day Worship*, pp. 32, 36.

rest of the NT Apostles and understand why the Sabbath was never given much attention in their writings. **They all understood it to have been a mere <u>sign</u> that pointed forward to Christ as the Reality and True Giver of rest and redemption (Matt. 11:28-30; Luke 19:9-10; 24:21), and therefore, continuing to hold onto it and promoting it in its "external rites" after His arrival, would be tantamount to denying His having come.** Edersheim, like O'Hare, catches the 'redemptive rest' that the Sabbath signified:

> But this was not the only rest to which the Sabbath pointed. There is also a rest of redemption, and the Sabbath was expressly connected with the deliverance of Israel from Egypt. 'Remember that thou was a servant in the land of Egypt, and that Jehovah thy God brought thee out thence through a mighty hand and by a stretched out arm: therefore Jehovah thy God commanded thee to keep the Sabbath-day' (Deut. 5:15). At the close of the work-a-day week, holy rest in the Lord; at the end of the labor and sorrow of Egypt, redemption and rest; and both pointing forward to the better rest (Heb. 4:9), and ultimately to the eternal Sabbath of completed work, of completed redemption, and completed 'hallowing' (Rev. 11)- was the meaning of the weekly Sabbath.[70]

Redemption in Christ is a consistent theme in the New Testament. Galatians 3:13 says that, "Christ redeemed us from the curse of the law by becoming a curse for us." In 4:4-5 we read, "But when the fullness of time had come, God sent forth his Son, born of woman, born under the law, to redeem those who were under the law, so that we might receive adoption as sons." Paul was equally emphatic in Ephesians 1, "In him we have redemption through his blood, the forgiveness of our trespasses, according to the riches of his grace" (vs. 7). In Titus 2:14, he did not fail to mention that Jesus "gave himself for us to redeem us from all lawlessness and to purify for himself a people for his own possession who are zealous for good works." The Apostle Peter was equally convinced that believers have been redeemed in

---

[70] Alfred Edersheim, *The Temple - Its Ministry and Service*, Chapter 9 – "Sabbath in the Temple," n.p. (accessed on *The Word* Bible Software)

Jesus and he sought to remind them that this redemption did not happen with "corruptible things" but with Jesus' precious blood. In 1 Peter 1:18-19 we read, "knowing that you were not redeemed with corruptible things, like silver or gold, from your futile way of life handed down from your forefathers, but with the precious blood of Christ, as of a lamb blameless and spotless." (EMTV). The Apostle John, in the book of Revelation, convincingly mentions that God/Christ redeemed His people (Rev. 5:9; 14:3, 4).

As a result of this redemptive theme that was foreshadowed in the Sabbath being fulfilled in Christ, we can appreciate that the Apostles and NT writers focused on the Reality and the redemption He provided rather than on the faint shadow. The shadow had to give way to the Substance and wane in importance. And because the Sabbath is no longer the focus by virtue of the coming of the Reality, the keeping of it would no longer be mandatory as it was under the Old Covenant. The Apostles seemed to have grasped this very quickly. So, what now mattered to them was not the mere keeping of a day, but the 'keeping' of a Person—Jesus Christ, as He is the quintessential Sabbath: He is Redemption. Dr. Clinton Baldwin concurs, "Fundamentally, genuine Sabbath-keeping means not only resting on a day, but at a deeper level it means resting in a person-Jesus Christ. The Sabbath is more than a day, it is a Person-Jesus Christ Himself."[71] Greg Taylor, commenting on Luke 4:16-21, notes profoundly:

> Jesus not only claimed to be the Messiah in this statement, but He called himself the *Jubilee*! Jesus called Himself the *Ultimate Sabbath*! He was claiming to be the Messiah and the Sabbath personified. The people knew exactly what He was claiming! They tried to kill Him for it. Can

---

[71] Clinton Baldwin, *The Sabbath: More Than a Day- A Person* (Spanish Town, JAM: Lithomedia Printers Limited, 2012), p. 63.

Jesus be any more clear about who He is? The Sabbath is a Person![72]

Unlike the Old Covenant Sabbath that could only be kept once a week on the seventh day, the New Covenant Sabbath rest (Jesus Christ) can be 'kept' seven days a week for the entirety of a believer's earthly pilgrimage. Teresa and Arthur Beem point out that Christ took the Sabbath of the Jews and made it a daily rest of faith for all mankind. They provide this analysis:

> ...if Jesus meant literally that the Sabbath was made for mankind, it was to teach that Christ was opening up the New Covenant Sabbath for all. He was taking this rest that had been meant for the Jews, and giving it as a forever Sabbath to all believers—Jew and gentile. It was an introduction to the daily Sabbath *rest of faith*: Jesus being the axis between the weekly Sabbath of flesh and the new moment by moment Sabbath of the Spirit. If Christ is indeed our spiritual rest, then he has become the Sabbath for all mankind and not just the Jew.[73]

Such understanding is the thrust of Hebrews chapters 3 and 4 where God's rest and redemption is discussed. God's "rest" of redemption and salvation in Jesus is said to can be entered into "Today", that is, whenever we hear the gospel and believe it (4:2-3, 6-7). The author then went on to state that God's rest has been standing from the creation of the world (4:3) and it remains for some to enter into "Today" (4:6, 9). In 4:9 the Greek word for "rest"- σαββατισμος (*sabbatismos*),[74] meaning "a Sabbath-rest, a

[72] Greg Taylor, *Discovering the New Covenant* (Glendale, AZ: LAM Publications, LLC, 2004), p. 109. (emphasis in original)

[73] Teresa and Arthur Beem, *It's Okay NOT to be a Seventh-day Adventist: The Untold History and the Doctrine that Attempts to Repair the Temple Veil* (North Charleston, SC: BookSurge Publishing, 2008), pp. 184-185. (emphasis in original)

[74] Gerhard F. Hasel states, "Hebrews 4:9 states, "There remains therefore a Sabbath rest for the people of God." The words "sabbath rest" translate the Gk. noun *sabbatismos*, a unique word in the NT. This term appears also in Plutarch (Superst. 3 [Moralia 166a]) for Sabbath observance, and in four post-canonical Christian writings which are not dependent on Heb. 4:9 (Justin Dial. 23:3; Epiph. Panar. haer. 30, 2.2; *Martyrdom of Peter and Paul*, chap. 1; *Const. Apost.*

Sabbath-keeping," is misunderstood by Sabbatarians, in that, they think that this text is calling for New Covenant believers to literally keep the weekly Sabbath. But such an interpretation is far from what is revealed in the text. Here are some reasons that this text is not calling for a literal weekly Sabbath-keeping: **(1)** The rest that Hebrews 3 and 4 is speaking about is God's rest after Creation, not the seventh-day Sabbath (4:4; cf. Gen. 2:1-3). **(2)** God's rest of creation remains to this day for us to enter into (4:6). **(3)** The majority of the Israelites in the time of Joshua and David (who kept the Sabbath and all the other feasts) failed to enter into God's rest because of a lack of faith and disobedience (3:16-4:2, 6-8). **(4)** The Book of Hebrews was written to an audience of Jewish Christians who were still keeping the Sabbath and the feasts, and despite this could have failed to enter God's rest if they lacked faith or were disobedient. (vs. 1, 2, 11). **(5)** God's rest is entered

---

2.36.2) for seventh-day "sabbath celebration" (Hofius 1970:103–5). The author of Hebrews affirms in Heb. 4:3–11, through the joining of quotations from Gen. 2:2 and Ps 95:7, that the promised "sabbath rest" still anticipates a complete realization "for the people of God" in the eschatological end-time which had been inaugurated with the appearance of Jesus (1:1–3). "Sabbath rest" within this context is not equated with a future, post-eschaton Sabbath celebration in the heavenly sanctuary; it is likewise not experienced in the rest that comes in death. The experience of "sabbath rest" points to a present "rest" (*katapausis*) reality in which those "who have believed are entering" (4:3) and it points to a future "rest" reality (4:11). Physical sabbath-keeping on the part of the new covenant believer as affirmed by "sabbath rest" epitomizes cessation from "works" (4:10) in commemoration of God's rest at creation (4:4 = Gen 2:2) and manifests faith in the salvation provided by Christ. Heb. 4:3–11 affirms that physical "sabbath rest" (*sabbatismos*) is the weekly outward manifestation of the inner experience of spiritual rest (*katapausis*) in which the final eschatological rest is proleptically experienced already "today" (4:7). Thus "Sabbath rest" combines in itself Creation-commemoration, salvation-experience, and eschaton-anticipation as the community of faith moves toward the final consummation of total restoration and rest." (Gerhard F. Hasel, "Sabbath," in vol. 5, *The Anchor Yale Bible Dictionary*, ed. David Noel Freedman (New York: Doubleday, 1992), pp. 855-56.)

into by faith, when we hear the Gospel and believe it (4:1-3). **(6)** The phrase "another day" (4:8) and the constant refrain, "Today,"[75] means that whenever we hear the Gospel and believe, we immediately enter into God's rest (3:7, 13, 15; 4:7). It would be absurd to think that this can happen *only once a week*, on the Sabbath. **(7)** The one who _has entered_ into God's rest _has ceased_ from his works just as God _did_ from His.

Point number 7 provides strong, compelling evidence that these passages are not talking about literal Sabbath-keeping, but some elaboration is necessary to demonstrate this fact. The two aorist verbs in 4:10 in the Greek contain profound nuggets. The verb "has entered" is the Gr. εἰσελθὼν (*eiselthon*- second aorist active participle) and "has rested" is the Gr. κατέπαυσεν (*katepausen*-aorist active indicative). The aorist tense in the Greek speaks to instantaneous action, whether in the past, present, or future. In this passage, the aorist tense is referring to past action—when one "heard the gospel and believed" (vs. 2-3)—indicating that one instantly entered into God's rest at that time. Both verbs are in the active voice, which means that the action was performed by the subject with continued effect—ongoing, habitual state. To put it all together, what this means is that when one heard the Gospel and believed it, one instantaneously entered into God's rest and one continues to abide in that state of rest. That's what those two aorist verbs are connoting! And one ceased from one's own works as God *did* (past) from His, not as God *does* (present repetitive continuous). God worked for six days and **_rested once and for all_** from His work; His rest is not a cyclical, once-a-week rest. God has been resting from the time of His initial rest (Gen. 2:1-3) and He continues to abide in that state of rest to this day and ad infinitum. So too, like God, when we hear the Gospel and believe

---

[75] The Greek word σημερον (*semeron*)-"Today"- means "this very day/night" and speaks to the instant, moment, day, night, time, etc., when something has happened, is happening, or when one wants it to happen (Matt. 6:11; 11:23; 27:8; Luke 19:5; 22:34, 43; Acts 19:40; Rom. 11:8; 2 Cor. 3:14-15, etc.)

it, we enter into His rest once and for all and remain in that state of rest. This is the σαββατισμος—"Sabbath-keeping"—that Hebrews 4 encourages the believer to keep and to enter into. Michael Morrison puts it nicely:

> Why does he call this a Sabbath-rest? He is not slipping in a command for the seventh day Sabbath. That would be totally out of context. His exhortation throughout this book is telling Jewish people to look to Jesus. He is not urging them to do a better job of keeping Jewish customs that they were already keeping. The ancient Israelites, who had the Sabbath, did not enter the rest he is talking about. God's rest is entered by faith — by believing the Gospel (verses 3-4). The author is not interested in a day of the week — he is concerned about how people respond to Jesus. A person who keeps the weekly Sabbath but rejects Christ has not entered God's rest. We enter God's rest only by believing the Gospel of Jesus Christ. Why then does he call this a Sabbath rest? By using this word [σαββατισμος], he indicates that this is what the Sabbath pointed to. Just as the bronze snake pointed to Jesus' crucifixion (John 3:14), and the washings pointed to forgiveness, and the sacrifices pointed to Jesus, similarly, the weekly Sabbath pointed to something spiritual: our rest through faith in Christ. It is available — we may enter God's rest. Don't put it off — do it today.[76]

Furthermore, Hebrews 4:9-10 could not have been telling us to "keep the Sabbath" once a week as God does because *God does not keep the Sabbath*—not once a week—not at all, never (John 5:15-20). If God were to cease working for one day or keep one Sabbath, the universe would immediately collapse and everything would instantaneously die (Acts 17:28; Col. 1:15-17; Heb. 1:3). Therefore, the Sabbatarian who uses Hebrews 3 and 4 as an argument for literal and mandatory Sabbath-keeping is theologically and linguistically misguided. The thrust of these passages is saving rest and redemption in Christ now and the anticipation of the eternal rest to come later.

---

[76] Michael Morrison, *Sabbath, Circumcision, and Tithing: Which Old Testament Laws Apply to Christians?* 4th ed. (Arcadia, CA: Michael Morrison, 2002, 2003), p. 106.

Paul clearly teaches that Christians are free to keep or not to keep the Sabbath. Although this concept may seem strange to Christians who fully understand the implications of the Gospel, they are not free to condemn Sabbath-keepers simply because they have chosen to do so. Paul's revelation of the freedom that Christians find in the gospel takes such burdens off of the Body of Christ. The principle that we are permitted to esteem any day or not to esteem any day seems to be his way of teaching us that in essence, every day with Jesus in our hearts is the Sabbath because Jesus is our Sabbath. On the other hand, it would seem that Paul's sentiment would be properly represented by saying that he taught that individuals who teach mandatory Sabbath-keeping would be following in the footsteps of the heretical Judaizers. Further evidence that this view is correct is the fact that Paul spent a great amount of time fighting the Judaizing heresy in the apostolic church (Acts 15; the Book of Galatians; Col. 2; Titus 1; etc.,).

Paul teaches that Sabbath observance is a matter of personal conviction. Believers may feel free to keep the seventh-day Sabbath, keep any other day of the week, or not keep any day at all. What matters is not what "day" we keep, but Who we "keep"—Jesus Christ. A logical extension of Paul's teaching about "days" would be that as we "keep" Jesus, the Real Sabbath, in our hearts, His Presence there "keeps" every day of our lives as a true spiritual rest that we could never achieve in our own power.

(B) The Sabbath is a ceremonial law.

Ceremonial laws can be defined as "the ceremonies and rituals of the Mosaic Law that served to show God's holiness and to keep Israel holy and distinct from gentiles, which also foreshadowed Christ and His work."[77] This definition can be corroborated with Colossians 2:16-17, Hebrews 9:9-10 and 10:1-4. Paul Enns defines

---

[77] My personal definition

ceremonial law simply as that "which legislated Israel's worship life."[78] Ferdinand Schenck was a bit more descriptive, "The ceremonial law taught of the holiness of God and of a coming Savior, and was designed to provide for the restored obedience to the moral law."[79] But however one chooses to define the "ceremonial law,"[80] there are certain things that the Bible student should not miss about it: **(1)** it is not intrinsically moral—only rituals about worship that are designed to teach holiness. **(2)** It contains shadows pointing to a Greater Reality. **(3)** It is temporary and can be suspended, dismissed, and sidestepped to fulfil moral obligations, and it can eventually be abrogated when it becomes meaningless or when it meets its Reality. More could have been listed but these are sufficient. The question that gnaws at us now is, does the Sabbath fall into the category of moral law or ceremonial law? This question is answered with precision and clarity by Michael Morrison:

> Jesus consistently compared the Sabbath with ritual laws, not the laws about the way we should treat our neighbors. Those ritual laws showed us how to worship God, how to express love to him. We might assume that these laws are the most important and the most permanent, but the opposite is true: The laws of worship are precisely the laws most likely to be obsolete. All those sacrifices and rituals, specifying this and that, are done away in Christ. We do not have to

---

[78] Paul P. Enns, *The Moody Handbook of Theology* (Chicago, IL: Moody Press, 1989), p. 639.

[79] Ferdinand S. Schenck, *The Ten Commandments and the Lord's Prayer* (New York: Funk & Wagnalls, 1902), p. 11.

[80] The designation of biblical laws as "moral law," "civil law," "statute law," "ceremonial law," etc., are not resident in the Bible itself. These are terms assigned to the various biblical laws by Bible scholars and students based on a number of factors; such as, the nature of the precepts, and the ground on which they rest, or the reason why they are obligatory, etc. For a good treatment of this see Charles Hodge, vol. 3, *Systematic Theology* (Oak Harbor, WA: Logos Research Systems, Inc., 1997), pp. 267-269.

show love to God in exactly the same way as the Israelites did. We find additional evidence that the Sabbath is a ritual law in that God himself does not keep the Sabbath. It is not part of His nature. He rested once, but a six-one cycle is not part of his eternal nature. Nor do we have any evidence that angels keep the Sabbath; it was not designed for them. This means that the Sabbath is not an inherent part of the way good creatures show love to God or to one another. The Sabbath is not eternal, for it did not exist before creation, and will not be relevant in the new heavens and new earth. The Sabbath is not God's nature, nor universal, nor timeless. It is a ritual law, saying that behavior that is good on Friday is not good on Saturday. Good angels always worship God, they never make idols, and they never misuse God's name. They always honor the Father, never murder, steal, commit adultery, steal or covet. (They cannot commit adultery because they are sexless, but they would not commit adultery even if they could.) They are in literal compliance with nine of the Ten Commandments, and will forever be in compliance with those nine, but they do not keep the Sabbath. This also shows that the Sabbath is different from the other nine commandments. It is different in quality—a ceremonial law rather than a moral law. Morality does not depend on the rotation of the earth, the day of the week, etc. Jesus clearly ranked the showbread as more important than the Sabbath, and the temple sacrifices as more important than the Sabbath, and circumcision as more important than the Sabbath. Jesus said that the Sabbath had to be broken so that sacrifices and circumcision could be performed — but I can't imagine Jesus saying that an important law had to be broken so a ritual could be performed! Clearly, the Sabbath law is a ritual law. It should be no surprise that the Sabbath command expired at the same time as those other commands.[81]

Morrison, proverbially, hit the nail on the head! The Sabbath is a ceremonial, ritual law that had foreshadowed Christ. And it lost most of its purpose and binding nature once Christ came, just like the ordinance of circumcision, sacrifices, food and drink offerings, purification rites, special dress codes, tithing, etc. A potent observation that further proves that the Sabbath is a ceremonial law is the fact that it can be suspended, dismissed, sidestepped,

---

[81] Morrison, *Sabbath, Circumcision, and Tithing: Which Old Testament Laws Apply to Christians?* 4th ed., p. 80.

and even abrogated by God when its observance becomes meaningless. In Isaiah 1:13-14, God dismissed the Sabbath, along with all of Israel's other feasts and new moons, because it lost its meaning as a result of their wickedness (cf. Amos 5:21-24). In Jeremiah's time and the Babylonian captivity, it was suspended, "forgotten" (NKJV), because of God's anger (Lam. 2:6). In Hosea 2:11, God promised to abolish all of Israel feasts, new moons, and Sabbaths. Countless accounts of Jesus' actions in the Gospels reveal how many times He sidestepped the Sabbath, allowed others to do so, or taught that others did so with impunity (Matt. 12:1-14; Mark 2:23-28; John 5:5-20; 7:21-24; and 9:1-16). These examples reveal the ceremonial nature of the Sabbath. We never read in Scripture where God suspended, dismissed, sidestepped or abrogated moral commands or approved of His people doing so, yet we see this often with the Sabbath.

And if these evidences do not convince one of the ceremonial nature of the Sabbath, the fact that Paul reduced its significance to a mere "shadow" should suffice. In Colossians 2:16-17, Paul said, "Therefore let no one pass judgment on you in questions of food and drink, or with regard to a festival or a new moon or a Sabbath. These are a shadow of the things to come, but the substance belongs to Christ." Adventists and other Sabbatarians try to dance around this text by claiming that "Sabbath" here is a reference to the "ceremonial Sabbaths." The *Seventh-day Adventist Bible Commentary* comments, "...the "sabbath days" Paul declares to be shadows pointing to Christ cannot refer to the weekly Sabbath designated by the fourth commandment, but must indicate the ceremonial rest days that reach their realization in Christ and His kingdom."[82] But no matter how much they dance, this is a reference to the weekly Sabbath. Bacchiocchi, to

---

[82] Nichol, *The Seventh-day Adventist Bible Commentary: The Holy Bible With Exegetical and Expository Comment.*, Commentary Reference Series, pp. 205-206.

my surprise, confessed this and criticized his own Church's Bible commentary for the linguistic distortion of this text. He states:

The sacred times prescribed by the false teachers are referred to as "a festival or a new moon or a sabbath– *eortes he neomenia he sabbaton*" [sic] (2:16). The unanimous consensus of commentators is that these three words represent a logical and progressive sequence (annual, monthly and weekly) as well as an exhaustive enumeration of the sacred times. This view is validated by the occurrence of these terms, in similar or reverse sequence, five times in the Septuagint and several times in other literature. There is, however, an exceptional occurrence in Isaiah 1:13-14 where the "new moon" is found at the beginning of the enumeration rather than in the middle, but an exception does not invalidate a common usage. The *Seventh-day Adventist Bible Commentary* interprets the *"sabbaton*–sabbath days" as a reference to the annual ceremonial Sabbaths and not to the weekly Sabbath (Lev. 23-6-8, 15, 16, 21, 24, 25, 27, 28, 37, 38). It is a fact that both the Sabbath and the Day of Atonement in Hebrew are designated by the compound expression *shabbath shabbathon*, meaning "a sabbath of solemn rest" (Ex. 31:15; 35:2; Lev. 23:3, 32; 16:31). But this phrase is rendered in the Septuagint by the compound Greek expression *sabbata sabbaton* which is different from the simple *sabbaton* found in Colossians 2:16. It is therefore linguistically impossible to interpret the latter as a reference to the Day of Atonement or to any other ceremonial sabbaths, since these are never designated simply as *sabbata*. The *SDA Bible Commentary* rests its interpretation, however, not on the grammatical and linguistic use of the word *sabbaton* but rather on a theological interpretation of the Sabbath as related to 'shadow' in Colossians 2:17. It is argued that "the weekly Sabbath is a memorial of an event at the beginning of earth's history... hence the "sabbath days" Paul declares to be shadows pointing to Christ cannot refer to the weekly Sabbath..., but must indicate the ceremonial rest days that reach their realization in Christ and His Kingdom." To determine the meaning of a word exclusively by theological assumptions, rather than by linguistic or contextual evidences, is against the canons of Biblical hermeneutics. Moreover even the theological interpretation which the Adventist commentary gives to the Sabbath is hard to justify, since we have seen that the Sabbath can legitimately be regarded as the "shadow" or fitting symbol of the present and future blessing of salvation.[83]

Despite this profound assessment and confession, Bacchiocchi still maintained that mandatory Sabbath-keeping is not jeopardized in Colossians 2. He continued:

> In view of the prevailing astral superstitions which influenced the observance of days among both Jews and pagans, it seems plausible to assume that any Sabbath observance advocated by the Colossians' ascetic teachers—known for their promotion of the worship of the elements of the universe—could only have been of a rigorous and superstitious type. A warning against such a type of Sabbath-keeping by the Apostle would have been not only appropriate but also desirable. But in this case Paul would be attacking not the principle of Sabbath-keeping but its perversion. Observe, however, that the Apostle is not admonishing against the *form* of these observances, but against their perverted *function*. The *manner* in which a Christian eats, drinks, or observes days and seasons is (as well stated in Romans 14:5) a matter of personal conviction to be respected, but the *motivation* for observing them is not a matter of personal viewpoint. These observances are and must remain a shadow pointing to the substance which belongs to Christ and must never become the substitute for the reality. It is not therefore the *form or manner* of observance of sacred times that Paul opposes but their perverted *function* and *motivations,* which adulterated the ground of salvation.[84]

Bacchiocchi's conclusion is that Paul is not opposing the observance of these four key Jewish ordinances in and of themselves, but merely is objecting to the perverted utilization of them by the Judaizers. However, this conclusion is very problematic on several levels. Paul states that these dietary laws, annual festivals, new moon celebrations, and Sabbaths are shadows that pointed forward to Christ. If Paul is not opposing these ordinances, but merely their "perverted function and motivations," we should be able to test Bacchiocchi's claims by subjecting them to the test of logic.

---

[83] Bacchiocchi, *From Sabbath to Sunday*, pp. 338-339.
[84] Ibid, p. 342. (emphasis in original)

More precisely, by the rules of logic, if what Bacchiocchi claims is true, then Paul is telling the Colossian Christians not to let the heretical ascetics judge them for not keeping the "perverted" forms of these ordinances. This is something that Paul would not do.

In the first place, observe that taking Bacchiocchi's argument to its furthest possible point results in the creation of an unintended heresy. That is, the perverted times and seasons are shadows of Christ and of things to come. **Contrariwise, perverted seasons and Sabbaths *could have never been nor will they ever* be a shadow of things to come, much less of Christ!** Because we are immediately stopped by this heretical barrier, we are placed in a position where we have little choice but to conclude that Paul was referring to the ordinances themselves, which did serve as symbolic representation of things that were to come, and especially to Christ's death on the Cross. And if it can be shown that this conclusion is accurate, it would fit well with his instruction in Romans 14:5 that "Each one should be fully convinced in his own mind" in whether to keep them or not, because the shadow has become unimportant ipso facto that the Reality (Jesus Christ) *has come.* These four ordinances are cornerstones of the Law of Moses. The reason Paul gives us for their obsolescence is that the Law of Moses perished at the Cross. When these ordinances became obsolete, any additional rules and regulations vanished with them. Let us examine an assortment of reasons why the Mosaic Law is in view in Colossians 2 and why these things have vanished.

Even though the customary Greek word for the Mosaic Law, voμoς (*nomos*), is not used in this passage (nor in the entire book for that matter), key terms and references tell us that it is referring to it. Terms such as circumcision and uncircumcision (vs. 11, 13; cf. Gen. 17:9-14; Exo. 12:43-49; Lev. 12:2-3; Eze. 44:5-9; Acts 15:1, 5; Gal. 5:2-3); sins and trespasses (vs. 11, 13; cf. Rom.

4:13-15; 5:19-20; Gal. 3:17-24); food, drink, festival, new moon, and Sabbath (vs. 16; cf. Num. 28, 29); dietary restrictions (vs. 16, 21-23, cf. Lev. 11; Num. 6; Deut. 14); and "a shadow of things to come"(vs. 17). As a matter of fact, "a shadow of things to come" is a similar statement we read in Hebrews 10:1 concerning the Mosaic Law: "...the law has but a shadow of the good things to come...." And the profound reference and conclusion that "the substance belongs to Christ" (vs. 17). This last reference echoes John 5:39-47 where Jesus said that the Mosaic Law testified about Him and that He is its Substance. (This same concept also surfaces in Luke 24:25-27, 44-47.) With all these things in mind, we can see that the abrogation of the Law of Moses is indicated by the content of Colossians 2. We are now ready to examine verses 16-17 to ascertain if the weekly Sabbath is what is being referenced as a "shadow" that has lost its litigious claw by the advent of Jesus.

There are two main arguments that Adventists and other Sabbatarians utilize today to deflect the weekly Sabbath in these two verses: **(1)** The mention of "food and drink" refers to the "ceremonial Sabbaths" because those items were offered on them and not on the weekly Sabbath, and **(2)** The plural form in the Greek "σαββατων" (rendered "the Sabbath *days*" (KJV), "Sabbaths" (NKJV), "Sabbath days" (NET), etc.) refers to the yearly ceremonial Sabbaths.

With regards to the first argument, it shows a lack of comprehensive biblical knowledge because, in fact, "food and drink" were offered on the Sabbath—every Sabbath. In Numbers 28:9-10 we read, "On the Sabbath day, two male lambs a year old without blemish, and two tenths of an ephah of fine flour for a grain offering, mixed with oil, and its drink offering: this is the burnt offering of every Sabbath, besides the regular burnt offering and its drink offering." In the Book of Ezekiel we read, "It shall be the prince's duty to furnish the burnt offerings, grain offerings, and drink offerings, at the feasts, the new moons, and the Sabbaths, all the appointed feasts of the house of Israel: he shall provide the sin offerings, grain offerings, burnt offerings, and peace offerings, to make atonement on behalf of the house of Israel." (45:17). In Ezekiel 46, we observe further:

> Thus says the Lord GOD: The gate of the inner court that faces east shall be shut on the six working days, but on the Sabbath day it shall be opened, and on the day of the new moon it shall be opened. The prince shall enter by the vestibule of the gate from outside, and shall take his stand by the post of the gate. The priests shall offer his burnt offering and his peace offerings, and he shall worship at the threshold of the gate. Then he shall go out, but the gate shall not be shut until evening. The people of the land shall bow down at the entrance of that gate before the LORD on the Sabbaths and on the new moons. The burnt offering that the prince offers to the LORD on the Sabbath day shall be six lambs without blemish and a ram without blemish. And the grain offering with the ram shall be an ephah, and the grain offering with the lambs shall be as much as he is able, together with a hin of oil to each ephah (vs. 1-5).

These special sacrifices on the weekly Sabbath clearly demonstrate that the first argument has no biblical foundation, was hastily concluded, and refutes the Adventist view that the weekly Sabbath is different from the others with regards to the "food and drink" requirement and it not being a foreshadow of Christ.

The second argument that contends that the plural form σαββατων (sabbaton) in the Greek refers to the yearly festivals collapses. Undoubtedly, this approach collapses for a number of reasons. Firstly, linguistically speaking, even though the yearly Sabbaths are called "Sabbaths" (KJV)[85] in the Old Testament (Lev.

---

[85] The KJV's rendition of the yearly Sabbaths as "Sabbaths" should be understood as "rest." The LXX does not use σαββατον in reference to these "Sabbaths" (with the exception of the compound σαββατα σαββατων for the Day of Atonement (Lev. 16:31; 23:32), as was also pointed out by Bacchiocchi), it uses ἀνάπαυσις (anapausis) meaning "rest," to designate them.

23:6–8, 15, 16, 21, 24, 25, 27, 28, 37, 38, etc.), they are *never designated* as such in the New Testament. In other words, *sabbaton* is never used to refer to the yearly Sabbaths in the New Testament. All the other Sabbaths of Israel are either always referred to by name or alluded to by what characterized them, by how they are fulfilled in Christ and/or by how they are reinterpreted in the New Testament.[86, 87] Only the weekly Sabbath is always called *sabbaton* in the New Testament.[88] The word *sabbaton*, whether used in the singular or plural, always has something to do with the numerical concept of "sevens." Therefore, in some cases *sabbaton* is used in the New Testament to refer to the "Sabbath" week of seven days,[89] with the Sabbath

---

[86] New Moon (Col. 2:16), Passover (Matt. 26:2, 17; Acts 12:4; John 18:18; 1 Cor. 5:7; Heb. 11:28, etc.), Feast of Weeks or Pentecost (Acts 2:1; 20:16; 1 Cor. 16:8), Feast of Trumpets (Matt. 24:31; 1 Thess. 4:16; Rev. 8-9), Unleavened Bread (Matt. 16:6-12; 26:17; Mark 14:1, 12; Acts 12:3; 20:6; 1 Cor. 5:6-8; Gal. 5:9), Day of Atonement (Matt. 27:51; Mark 15:38; Luke 23:45; Rom. 3:25-26; Heb. 9:7-10), Feast of Tabernacles/Booths or Ingathering (John 7:2-10, 37-39; 2 Cor. 5:1-4; 2 Pet. 1:13-14; John 1:14; Rev. 21:3-5), First Fruits (1 Cor. 15:20-23; 16:15; Rom. 8:23; 16:5; James 1:18), Feast of Dedication/Hanukkah or Lights (John 10:22–23).

[87] For a lengthy discussion on and justification of these facts, see Robert Webber, vol. 1, *The Biblical Foundations of Christian Worship*, 1st ed., The Complete Library of Christian Worship (Nashville, TN: Star Song Pub. Group, 1993), pp. 182-192.

[88] σάββατον [*sabbaton /sab·bat·on/*] neuter noun, Of Hebrew origin 7676; TDNT 7:1; TDNTA 989; Gr. 4879; 68 occurrences; AV translates as "sabbath day" 37 times, "sabbath" 22 times, and "week" nine times. 1-the seventh day of each week which was a sacred festival on which the Israelites were required to abstain from all work. 1A -the institution of the Sabbath, the law for keeping holy every seventh day of the week. 1B - a single Sabbath, Sabbath day. 2-seven days, a week. (James Strong, *Enhanced Strong's Lexicon* (Woodside Bible Fellowship, 1995).

[89] Smick documents, "The next division of time, the week (shābûaʿ, meaning a heptad of days), was used throughout the biblical world from time immemorial. Yet it has no connection with astronomical phenomena. The biblical record clearly teaches that the origin of the week rests squarely on God's sovereign

being the chief day and even determining how the other days are called. For example, the first day of the week is called μίαν σαββάτων (*mian sabbaton*), "first day after the Sabbath"—"first day of the week" (Matt. 28:1; Mark 16:2; John 20:1; 20:19; Acts 20:7; 1 Cor. 16:1-2), this is the only one represented in the NT. However, historical Christian literature bear witness to this fact and contain the others. For example, in *The Didache* 8:1 we read, "αἱ δὲ νηστεῖαι ὑμῶν μὴ ἔστωσαν μετὰ τῶν ὑποκριτῶν· νηστεύουσι γὰρ δευτέρᾳ σαββάτων καὶ πέμπτῃ· ὑμεῖς δὲ νηστεύσατε τετράδα καὶ παρασκευήν." This is translated as, "But as for your fasts, let them not be with the hypocrites: for they fast on the second and fifth day of the week, but you are to fast on the fourth and the preparation day." (author's translation). In this Greek sentence, the days of the week are called as follows: δευτέρᾳ σαββάτων ("second day after the Sabbath"), πέμπτῃ σαββάτων[90] ("fifth day after the Sabbath"), τετραδα σαββατων ("fourth day after the Sabbath"), and the "sixth day after the Sabbath," which could have been designated as ἕκτην σαββατων, is called παρασκευήν, "preparation day," which was one of the standard names for the day before the Sabbath (Matt. 27:62; Mark 15:42; Luke 23:54; John 19:31, 42), with προσαββατον

---

choice to create all things in six days and to cease from His creative work the seventh, and His subsequent command to man to emulate Him in His labors. So the week as a divider of time was strictly a religious matter having no other basis. The period from sabbath to sabbath in the NT is called a sabbaton (Mt 28:1), which word derives from the Heb. shabbāt, meaning "rest," rather than sheba⁄ meaning "seven." The Israelites had other periods of time in their religious calendar which were based on the seven cycle, such as the seven sabbaths from the Day of Atonement to the Feast of Pentecost (Lev 23:15–16), and the seven heptads of years which measured the time of the year of jubilee when debts were cancelled and bond servants were freed (Lev 25:8 ff.). (Elmer B. Smick, "Time, Divisions Of" In, in *The Wycliffe Bible Encyclopedia*, ed. Charles F. Pfeiffer, Howard F. Vos and John Rea (Moody Press, 1975).)

[90] Σαββατων, though used once in the verse, is the static noun in the sentence that is being modified by the ordinal numbers "second, fifth, fourth, and sixth;" hence my repetition of it with the respective ordinal numbers for clarity.

(prosabbaton) ("the day before the Sabbath" – Mark 15:42) being the other.

Secondly, any attempt to evade the fact that Colossians 2:16-17 targets the weekly Sabbath of the Decalogue does not work because there are about 20 other places in the NT where the plural form of the word Sabbath (σαββατον) is used and context demands the meaning to be the weekly Sabbath. The Greeks didn't have the same concern over plural versus singular forms of words that is found in the English language. Of the 68 times the Greek NT uses the word σαββατον (*sabbaton*) in its various declension cases, whether in the singular or plural, with or without the definite article, it *always means* the weekly Sabbath. This fact is so obvious to NT Greek students, that I will use one passage to demonstrate this. In Matthew 12:1-12, the forms of σαββατον are used as follows: vs. 1- σάββασιν (dative plural), vs. 2- σαββάτῳ (dative singular), vs. 5- σάββασιν (dative plural) and σάββατον (accusative singular), vs. 8- σαββάτου (genitive singular), vs. 10-12- σάββασιν (dative plural). For the sake of showing it in all of its declining forms, it is in Mark 2:27 as σάββατον (nominative singular), Acts 17:2- σάββατα (accusative/nominative plural), and Luke 4:16- σαββάτων (genitive plural).

The sentence structure of this text (Col. 2:16) — festival, new moon, or Sabbath — is a phrase used in the OT to imply the three aspects of Jewish festival structure and designates the order of annual, monthly, and weekly festivals. This annual, monthly, and weekly sequence appears five times in the Septuagint in both ascending and descending order — i.e., 2 Chronicles 2:4, 31:3, Nehemiah 10:33, Ezekiel 45:17, and Hosea 2:11. All through the history of the Israelites there existed a consistent chain of annual Sabbaths, monthly new moon celebrations, and weekly Sabbaths. If the word Sabbath as used here means yearly Sabbaths, the sentence would read, "annual Sabbaths, monthly Sabbaths, and annual Sabbaths." This clearly would not make any sense because "festival" already encapsulates all the annual Sabbaths, and also the three-part Hebrew convention of referring to the appointed festivals as a three-part set, listing them according to how often they are scheduled (once a year, once a month, and every week) would be structurally and conventionally violated. Every time the Old Testament links the New Moon celebration with the Sabbath, as is in Colossians 2:16, the weekly Sabbath is what is always in view (2 Kings 4:23; 1 Chron. 23:31; 2 Chron. 2:4; 8:13; Neh. 10:33; Isa. 1:13; 66:23; Ezek. 45:17; 46:1; Hosea 2:11; and Amos 8:5). This proves beyond a shadow of doubt that the weekly Sabbath is what Paul is talking about here. Paul is clearly saying that dietary rules, the annual feasts, monthly feasts, and weekly Sabbaths are not to be made tests of Christian beliefs or practices. They are not issues of soul salvation. They are merely shadows of things that were[91] to come, but Christ is the present Reality—the Object Who

---

[91] The NIV and the Weymouth New Testament translate this clause as "were to come" and "were soon to come" respectively. While the Greek verb ἐστιν (estin) is in the present tense, those renderings are accurate. Here is the reason- "Some phrases which might be rendered as past tense in English will often occur in the present tense in Greek. These are termed "historical presents," and such occurrences dramatize the event described as if the reader were there watching the event occur. Some English translations render such historical presents in the English past tense, while others permit the tense to remain in the present." (Larry Pierce, *Tense Voice Mood* (Bellingham, WA: Logos Bible Software). A clear example of this is found in Romans 5:14 (ESV)- "Yet death reigned from Adam to Moses, even over those whose sinning was not like the transgression of Adam, who was a type of the one who was to come." The phrase "who was to come" in the Greek is "ὅς ἐστιν τύπος τοῦ μέλλοντος." Notice that the verb εστιν (estin) is in the present tense but that it is translated as the past tense. The translators almost certainly made this decision because Adam is not "to come." He had been dead for millennia at the writing of Romans. Paul wanted his readers to palpably experience the "historical present" as they "watch the event occur." As a matter of fact, this Greek phrase is identical to the one in Colossians 2:16- "ἅ ἐστιν σκιὰ τῶν μελλόντων" ("These are a shadow of the things to come") and both practically

94

created these shadows and to Whom they pointed.

Furthermore, from Greek word analysis, we have virtually conclusive evidence that the word Paul chose for the third position in his list of three holy days—σαββάτων (sabbatōn-neuter noun, genitive, plural) *always* refers to the weekly Sabbath in the New Testament (see the Greek of Matt. 28:1; Mark 16:2; Luke 4:16; Luke 24:1; John 20:1; 20:19; Acts 13:14; 16:13; 20:7 and 1 Cor. 16:2 (KJV Greek text) and also in the Septuagint. For example, Exodus 20:8 says, "Remember the Sabbath day [τὴν ἡμέραν τῶν σαββάτων] to keep it holy." Chapter 35:3 reads, "You shall kindle no fire in all your dwelling places on the Sabbath day [τῇ ἡμέρᾳ τῶν σαββάτων]." We read in Deuteronomy 5:12 and 15, "Observe the Sabbath day [τῇ ἡμέρᾳ τῶν σαββάτων], to keep it holy, as the LORD your God commanded you...Therefore the LORD your God commanded you to keep the Sabbath day [τῇ ἡμέρᾳ τῶν σαββάτων]. See also these OT passages for its use: Leviticus 23:15 and 24:8, Numbers 28:9-10, 2 Kings 16:18, 2 Chronicles 31:3, Nehemiah 10:33, Isaiah 58:13, Jeremiah 17:21-27, Ezekiel 22:26, and 46:1, 4, 12.

To this point, the weekly Sabbath has been demonstrated to be a mere shadow of the Reality of Christ. While the other Jewish ordinances were shadowy representations of Him in one way or another, the weekly Sabbath represented Christ in a spectacular manner. Every weekly Sabbath the Israelites witnessed the slaying

---

mean the same thing. The only differences in that in Romans 5:14 τύπος (*tupos*- "type") is used instead of σκια (*skia*- "shadow"), but both words are synonyms of each other. So to understand the festivals and Sabbath as shadows of things that "were to come" is accurate because Christ had already come. Also, to consider them as "to come" is also accurate because we anticipate the ultimate heavenly, eternal Sabbath rest that will begin at His Second Coming. Paul seemed to have deliberately written it this way to give his audience, both then and us now, a feeling that they are in the "historical present" as they read the Book of Colossians.

of two spotless lambs in addition to the other required sacrifices. This dramatic scene should have caused them to see the connection between these shadows and the death of the Spotless Lamb of God on the Cross. In view of this special symbolic connection, Paul's statement that the weekly Sabbath was an obsolete shadow should have been recognized by well-informed Israelites. The next logical step would be nearly self-evident. We should not judge fellow believers in regard to whether they observe a shadow or do not observe a shadow. D. R. de Lacey, in *From Sabbath to Lord's Day*, concluded on Colossians 2:16-17:

> As with the law, Paul's attitude to the festivals here seems to be that they have lost their intrinsic value but may be enjoyed by those who wish so to use them. However we interpret the situation, Paul's statement "Let no one pass judgment on you," indicates that no stringent regulations are to be laid down over the use of festivals. As is the case with the law, the Christian is no longer bound by external stipulations in the matter of festivals.[92]

In a similar vein, H. M. Riggle stated:

> The law, with all its ordinances and shadowing rites, expired with Christ upon the cross....Let no man judge you by the laws of that code which had served its time and purpose, and vanished away. The laws respecting meats are no longer to be bound upon our consciences, neither "holy day", law feast-days, etc., nor yet monthly feasts determined by the moon; yea, and let no man judge you of the "Sabbath-days." These "Sabbath-days" cannot be specially referred to annual or monthly Sabbaths, for such are included in the former specifications. They must, therefore, have special reference to the round of weekly Sabbaths. They are all nailed to the cross and taken away.[93]

---

[92]D. R. de Lacey, "The Sabbath/Sunday Question and the Law in the Pauline Corpus" in *From Sabbath to Lord's Day: A Biblical, Historical, and Theological Investigation*, edited by D. A. Carson (previously published by Zondervan, 1982). Reprinted (Eugene, Oregon: Wipf and Stock Publishers, 1999), p. 183.

[93] H. M. Riggle, *The Sabbath and the Lord's Day* (Guthrie, OK: Faith Publishing House, 1922; now published by LAM Publication, LLC, Glendale, AZ), p. 93.

This theological understanding of the Sabbath, no doubt, revolutionized Paul's mind, attitude, and theology; hence, his authoritative instruction regarding the same—"One person esteems one day as better than another, while another esteems all days alike. Each one should be fully convinced in his own mind. The one who observes the day, observes it in honor of the Lord...." (Rom. 14:5-6).

Troy W. Martin analyzed Colossians 2:16-17 from a novel perspective. He argues for the validity of the time-keeping system of this passage by virtue of their "relationship to the ultimate reality" and by their being used to "proclaim Christ." He states:

> Pauline thought recognizes that this temporal scheme is only a shadow of the reality to come. Nevertheless, worship according to this temporal system is valid even though it is only a shadow of future realities. Although he recognizes the absence of ultimate reality in the Christian time-keeping system, the Colossian author still argues for its validity because of its relationship to the ultimate reality. He exhorts the Colossians not to submit to the critique that their time-keeping scheme is useless, tyrannical or illusory. He urges them to ignore the accusation that the practice of festival, new moon and Sabbaths propagates false hopes and expectations about the future. He admonishes the Colossians, "Let no one critique you by your eating and drinking or in respect to your feast, new moon or Sabbaths which practices are a shadow of things to come but let everyone discern the body of Christ by your eating and drinking or in respect to your feast, new moon, or Sabbaths" (Col. 2.16-17). Instead of being on the defensive end of a poignant critique, this author encourages the Colossians to take the offensive and proclaim Christ to the critic by their Christian practices.[94]

This interpretation by Dr. Martin lends the understanding that Paul taught the Colossians not to let anyone judge them *for*

---

[94] Troy W. Martin, *By Philosophy and Empty Deceit: Colossians as Response to a Cynic Critique* (Sheffield, England: Sheffield Academic Press Ltd, 1996), pp. 133-134.

keeping the festivals and the weekly Sabbath. This Sabbatarian-friendly interpretation of Dr. Martin may lead some to believe he or she has found ammunition to mandate obligatory festival and Sabbath-keeping, but to the contrary, quite the opposite is achieved, as this interpretation buttresses what Paul says about "days" in Romans 14:5-6. That is, whether to keep them or not is based on personal conviction and is done in "honor of the Lord;" similar to Martin's conclusion that they are to "proclaim Christ to the critic by their Christian practices." The Christian who keeps the festivals and weekly Sabbaths still has *no right to judge or condemn* his brother who does not keep them and vice versa (Rom. 14:3-12). So, far from legislating mandatory festival and Sabbath observance, Martin's analysis of Colossians 2:14-17 reinforces and upholds Paul's call for Christian liberty as he articulates it in Romans 14:15-19. While Dr. Martin's interpretation *affirms* the concept that feast and Sabbath keeping is still necessary for New Covenant Christians, the natural reading of this passage (Col. 2:8-23) serves more to *negate* these Mosaic stipulations. For example, physical circumcision is negated because believers now have a spiritual circumcision and baptism in Christ (vs. 11-12). The believer's "record of debt" is negated and cancelled as a result of being forgiven by God (vs. 13-14). Food and drink regulations, and festivals are negated by having Christ as their Reality (vs. 16-17), and asceticism, food taboos and regulations are negated because believers have been "filled" in Christ and are dead to the elemental spirits of the world (vs. 18-23; cf. vs. 9-10). So while there may be some merit to Martin's analysis, that the observance of these ordinances is an affirmative option for believers, Paul's primary emphasis is their negation. **The crux of the matter is this, Christians are at liberty to eat or not to eat any animal, and they are free to observe or not to observe any day.** These Old Testament ordinances are no longer mandatory, no longer issues of salvation, and no longer eligible to qualify as points of contention among believers.

98

This is an illuminating statement by Michael Morrison.

The New Testament has space for all sorts of commands, from obvious things to subtle things, but it never commands the Sabbath. This would be odd if the Sabbath were an important command. We find sweeping statements that make the old covenant law obsolete, but unlike other commands, we never find the Sabbath commanded again or made an exception to the rule. Paul and John say a lot about the godly behavior that springs from Christian faith and love, but the Sabbath is simply never commanded. Paul dealt with numerous problems of Christian living, and he listed numerous sins that characterize people who will not inherit the kingdom of God, but he never mentions Sabbath breaking. In describing sins of the gentile (Romans 1), he says nothing about the Sabbath. If the Sabbath is essential, it is certainly surprising that no one is ever criticized for ignoring it. In the first-century Roman Empire, slaves would have found it particularly difficult to keep the Sabbath. Some of them had unconverted, harsh masters (1 Peter 2:18). Some parts of the Roman Empire didn't even use a seven-day week. But Peter and Paul did not have to answer questions about how slaves could keep the Sabbath. Why not? Because slaves didn't have to keep the Sabbath. For one thing, first century Jews did not believe that gentiles had to keep the Sabbath. For another, the decision at Jerusalem, recorded in Acts 15, was that converted, Spirit-filled gentiles were not required to become circumcised and keep the Law of Moses. Little is said about the Sabbath because it was not a problem. Instead, the Sabbath was a neutral matter, neither commanded nor forbidden. People were free to rest on that day if they chose, or to use the day in other ways, as long as they did what they did to the Lord (Romans 14:5-6). Likewise, the New Testament does not say that any other day ought to be a day of rest. There is no command to keep the first day, either as a day of meeting or a day of rest. It is neither commanded nor forbidden. Christians are free to work these things out for themselves. We are commanded to assemble together for worship, but we are not commanded when (Hebrews 10:25). The important thing is not which day we observe, but whether we have faith in Jesus Christ as Lord and Savior. He is the test commandment, the center of faith, the standard by which we will be judged. He is the answer to our deepest need.[95]

---

[95] Michael Morrison, p. 173.

Conclusion

Dr. Samuele Bacchiocchi and the Seventh-day Adventist Church have obfuscated the clear teachings of Romans 14 by theorizing that the reference to the dietary laws and "days" in this passage are to pagan dietary practices and to controversial fast days between Jews and Christians.

This book demonstrates beyond reasonable doubt from comprehensive Greek linguistic studies in the Septuagint that these references are clearly in regard to Jewish—not pagan—dietary laws and sacred days. Other scholars have utilized comparable methods to evaluate this question, but this study has examined the evidence from some new angles.

A total of three different perspectives indicates that it is virtually impossible that Paul would not be thinking of the most highly esteemed of all Jewish sacred days—the seventh-day Sabbath of the Decalogue—when he taught against esteeming one day above another in Romans 14:

(1) Evidence has been presented that demonstrates that Paul made clear references to the Law of Moses in Romans 14, specifically to two divisive issues—Levitical dietary rules and the Sabbath.

(2) Evidence has been presented from pagan culture and its religious practices during both Old and New Testament times which explains why Paul said that the "weak" believing Jews ate only vegetables and abstained from wine and meat, and were prone to judge their "strong" gentile brothers who partook of these things.

(3) A presentation of the similarities of New Testament Greek references to Jewish dietary laws and sacred days with the Greek references to Jewish dietary laws and sacred days in the Greek Old Testament (Septuagint) demonstrates beyond reasonable

doubt that the reference to the "day" in Romans 14 is to the Sabbath and not to pagan or Jewish "fast days" as presumed by Adventism. The correlation between the words for "clean and unclean" in Romans 14 with "clean and unclean" in Leviticus 11, Deuteronomy 14 and Acts 10, and a lexicological analysis of the usage of the word σαββατων in both Testaments is definitive.

These new insights further correlate with Paul's references to the Jewish dietary and holy days of Colossians 2 and buttress the fact that Paul really did teach that the Jewish dietary laws and Jewish sacred days were obsolete shadowy representations that perished when the Reality, that caused those shadows to exist, died on the Cross.

This study has demonstrated beyond any reasonable doubt that Paul clearly taught the Law of Moses was nailed to the Cross—an event which was absolutely necessary to bring an end to the need for Christian believers to concern themselves with any type of dietary restriction or holy day.

Christianity, then, cannot be about keeping the Sabbath, avoiding certain foods, and abstaining from wine. Under the New Covenant, these things are nonessential, non-salvific, and personal issues. The focus of the Kingdom of God is Christian love, unity in diversity, faith in Christ, and "...righteousness and peace and joy in the Holy Spirit." (Rom. 14:17). Conclusively, by being in Christ and His New Covenant, believers can rest assured that their salvation is not at stake with regards to these matters because *"All foods are clean and every day is the Sabbath."*

Selected Bibliography

Apocrypha: King James Version. Bellingham, WA: Logos Research Systems, Inc., 1995.

Bacchiocchi, Samuele. *From Sabbath to Sunday: A Historical Investigation of the Rise of Sunday Observance in Early Christianity* . Rome, Italy: The Pontifical Gregorian University Press, 1977.

_____. *The Sabbath in the New Testament: Answers to Questions.* Berrien Springs, MI: Biblical Perspectives, 2000.

_____. *The Sabbath Under Crossfire: A Biblical Analysis of Recent Sabbath/Sunday Developments.* Berrien Springs, MI: Biblical Perspectives, 1999.

Baldwin, Clinton. *The Sabbath: More Than a Day- A Person.* Spanish Town, JAM: Lithomedia Printers Limited, 2012.

Beem, Teresa and Arthur. *It's Okay NOT to be a Seventh-day Adventist: The Untold History and the Doctrine that Attempts to Repair the Temple Veil.* North Charleston, SC: BookSurge Publishing, 2008.

Cowan, Henry. "Literature, Sub-Apostolic", in *The International Standard Bible Encyclopaedia, Volumes 1–5*, ed. James Orr, John L. Nuelsen, Edgar Y. Mullins and Morris O. Evans. Chicago: The Howard-Severance Company, 1915.

Dunn, James D. G. vol. 38B, *Romans 9–16, Word Biblical Commentary.* Dallas: Word, Incorporated, 1998.

Edersheim, Alfred. *Sketches of Jewish Social Life,* chap. 2 "Jews and gentile in "The Land", n.p.ny. (accessed on *The Word* Bible Software)

_____. *The Temple - Its Ministry and Service*, chap. 9 "Sabbath in the Temple," n.p. ny. (accessed on *The Word* Bible Software)

Elwell, Walter A., and Walter A. Elwell, *Evangelical Dictionary of Biblical Theology*, electronic ed., Baker reference library. Grand Rapids: Baker Book House, 1996.

Enns, Paul P. *The Moody Handbook of Theology.* Chicago, IL: Moody Press, 1989.

Gladson, Jerry. *A Theologian's Journey from Seventh-day Adventism to Mainstream Christianity.* Glendale, AZ: LAM Publications, LLC, 2000.

Hasel, Gerhard F. "Sabbath", in vol. 5, *The Anchor Yale Bible Dictionary*, ed. David Noel Freedman. New York: Doubleday, 1992.

Jamieson, Robert, A. R. Fausset and David Brown, *Commentary Critical and Explanatory on the Whole Bible*. Oak Harbor, WA: Logos Research Systems, Inc., 1997.

Kraft, Robert A. "Didache", in vol. 2, *The Anchor Yale Bible Dictionary*, ed. David Noel Freedman. New York: Doubleday, 1992.

de Lacey, Douglas R. "The Sabbath/Sunday Question and the Law in the Pauline Corpus" in *From Sabbath to Lord's Day: A Biblical, Historical, and Theological Investigation*, ed. D. A. Carson. previously published by Zondervan, 1982; reprinted by Wipf and Stock Publishers, 1999, Eugene, OR.

MacArthur, Jr., John, ed. *The MacArthur Study Bible*, electronic ed. Nashville, TN: Word Pub., 1997.

Martin, Troy W. *By Philosophy and Empty Deceit: Colossians as Response to a Cynic Critique*. Sheffield, England: Sheffield Academic Press Ltd, 1996.

Ministerial Association General Conference of SDA, *Seventh-day Adventists Believe*. Boise, ID: Pacific Press Publishing Association, 1988, 2005.

Morrison, Michael. *Sabbath, Circumcision, and Tithing: Which Old Testament Laws Apply to Christians? 4th Ed.* Arcadia, CA: Michael Morrison, 2002, 2003.

Murphy, Edward F. *Handbook for Spiritual Warfare*. Nashville: Thomas Nelson, 1996.

Nichol, Francis D. *The Seventh-day Adventist Bible Commentary: The Holy Bible with Exegetical and Expository Comment., Commentary Reference Series*. Washington, D.C.: Review and Herald Publishing Association, 1978.

O'Hare, Terrence D. *The Sabbath Complete and the Ascendancy of First-Day Worship*. Eugene, OR: Wipf and Stock Publishers, 2011.

Packer, J. I., Merrill Chapin Tenney and William White, Jr. *Nelson's Illustrated Manners and Customs of the Bible*. Nashville, TN: Thomas Nelson, 1997.

Pierce, Larry. *Tense Voice Mood*. Bellingham, WA: Logos Bible Software.

Ratzlaff, Dale. *Sabbath in Christ*. Glendale, AZ: LAM Publications, LLC, 2010.

Riggle, H. M. *The Sabbath and the Lord's Day*. Guthrie, OK: Faith Publishing

House, 1922; now published by LAM Publication, LLC, Glendale, AZ.

Secretariat General Conference of Seventh-day Adventists. *Seventh-day Adventist Church Manual*, 19th Revised Ed. Nampa, ID: Pacific Press Publishing Association, 2016.

Schenck, Ferdinand S. *The Ten Commandments and the Lord's Prayer*. New York: Funk & Wagnalls, 1902.

Smick, Elmer B. "Time, Divisions Of", in *The Wycliffe Bible Encyclopedia*, ed. Charles F. Pfeiffer, Howard F. Vos and John Rea. Moody Press, 1975.

Strong, James. *Enhanced Strong's Lexicon*. Woodside Bible Fellowship, 1995.

Sweeney, James P. "Chronology of the New Testament", in *The Lexham Bible Dictionary*, ed. John D. Barry, David Bomar, Derek R. Brown et al. Bellingham, WA: Lexham Press, 2016.

Taylor, Greg. *Discovering the New Covenant*. Glendale, AZ: LAM Publications, LLC, 2004.

Unger, Merrill F. "Versions of the Scriptures", in *The New Unger's Bible Dictionary*, ed. R. K. Harrison, Rev. and updated ed. Chicago: Moody Press, 1988.

Weiss, Randall A. *Jewish Sects of the New Testament Era*. Cedar Hill, TX: Cross Talk, 1994.

Wesley, John. *Explanatory Notes Upon the Old Testament*, Volume 3. Bristol: William Pine, 1765.

White, Ellen G. *Counsels on Diet and Foods*. Washington, DC: Ellen G. White Estate, Inc., 2008.

_____.*Counsels on Health*. Washington, DC: Ellen G. White Estate, Inc., 2008.

_____. *Last Day Events*. Washington, DC: Ellen G. White Estate, Inc., 2008.

_____. *Review and Herald*, Dec. 20, 1898. Washington, DC: Ellen G. White Estate, Inc., 2008.

Zodhiates, Spiros. *The Complete Word Study Dictionary: New Testament*, electronic ed. Chattanooga, TN: AMG Publishers, 2000.

www.ingramcontent.com/pod-product-compliance
Lightning Source LLC
Chambersburg PA
CBHW072205090426
42740CB00012B/2396